D1196000

The Cultivation of

Community Leaders

The Cultivation of

Community Leaders

UP FROM THE GRASS ROOTS

By William W. Biddle

HARPER & BROTHERS PUBLISHERS

NEW YORK

Library of Congress catalog card number: 52-12037

TO LOUREIDE

Collaborator and Companion

Contents

PREFACE   ix

FOREWORD BY BAKER BROWNELL   xi

I. WHERE SHALL WE FIND OUR LEADERS?   I

II. EXPANDING THE CAMPUS   12

III. DISCOVERING COMMUNITIES   29

IV. TRAINING PARTICIPANT-LEADERS   43

V. TRAINING FUTURE CITIZENS   58

VI. TRAINING COMMUNITY EDUCATORS   73

VII. THE METHOD OF ENCOURAGEMENT   86

VIII. THE PROBLEM OF CONFLICT   101

IX. PARTICIPATIVE PUBLIC RELATIONS   119

X. THE DEMOCRATIZATION OF SOCIAL RESEARCH   135

XI. INDIVIDUAL AND GROUP   152

XII. A PRACTITIONER'S HANDBOOK   169

APPENDIX: A LIST OF HELPS   191

INDEX   201

Preface

This book is a preliminary record of a continuing experiment with the discovery and development of human potential in the community environment where men live. It is addressed to two kinds of people: first to the citizen-leaders, who can become stronger in self-directed zeal for the common good; second to the college teachers and administrators, who may realize their own possibilities in adapting their institutions to community need. The achievements are, as yet, humble and limited. But the fact that citizens and educators could cooperate to change themselves for the better in some small human laboratories promises much for the larger affairs of men.

Why the community as a place for joint experiment? Communities represent the manageable social unit for self-directed cooperation. In the modern day, mass man is pitted against democratic man. Mass man can be, and usually is, manipulated in huge hordes, on a nation-wide basis. Democratic man must live and grow within a smaller functioning group of his fellows. Perhaps much of democratic hope rests upon what happens in the habitat of free men, a self-determining community.

Why the small college as an initiator and encourager of the experiment? Too long these smaller centers of learning have sought futilely to imitate the great university, with smaller staffs, lesser facilities, and smaller budgets. Why should they not find their unique function in becoming promoters of democratic growth within the communities that lie close at hand? Perhaps thereby the American small college will do something which no university can do and contribute basically to a democracy revitalized at the grass roots.

There is a stirring among American communities. Optimists discover new vitality in democracy at the local level. Pessimists point out the weaknesses of inexperienced and timid leadership. This

book deals with leadership. It is offered to those who have already
spontaneously assumed responsibility, to those who see problems to
be solved but hesitate to push themselves forward, to those who
could be leaders with proper encouragement, but most of all to
those who would do the encouraging. The potential for leadership
is there, at the grass roots.

W. W. B.

Foreword

BY BAKER BROWNELL
Professor of Philosophy, Northwestern University

In this wise and canny book William W. Biddle interprets leadership—and the lack of it—as he sees it in the little places and elsewhere of America. It is fortunately a book for people, not for that strange deviant from the human race, the professional expert, and although Dr. Biddle clearly can toss about the expert's jargon when he wishes, his Quaker milieu at Earlham College, or the mid-American environment in which he does his work, or perhaps just a courteous impulse keeps the book friendly and simple. As such it is far more fundamental in its relation to this critical problem in our democracy than many volumes of stuffed shirt scholarship.

Ask any person concerned in the survival of the human community; ask for example Arthur E. Morgan, or Harry Schacter, Granville Hicks, Stanley Hamilton, Father Ligutti, or Richard Poston, H. C. Tate, Robert Gard, John Barton, Jess Ogden, Irwin Sanders or any other among those frontiersmen who have discovered in their American experience the sources of the rivers of our democratic life, and he probably will reply that the search for leadership and for ways to cultivate leadership in the small community has become the central purpose of his adventure.

In this book Dr. Biddle takes this problem directly to the colleges as well as to other appropriate places, and he says to them, "Why have you not faced this critical problem?" Nor does he stop there. He also asks, "What can you do to fulfill your profound obligation to society in this respect?" Then because the colleges and universities in general can give no answer to either question, he proceeds to answer them himself.

The answer given here is detailed, humble, humorous. It is illumined with his faith in the importance of the enterprise.

The Cultivation of

Community Leaders

CHAPTER I

Where Shall We
Find Our Leaders?

THE two-way conversation with a prominent community figure waxed warm. "I know where you and I are not understanding each other," said he. "You believe in people; I don't. You are willing to trust them to act as they should. I believe they must be forced to do the right thing."

"Yes," was the reply. "I believe in people. But not so much for what they are as for what they may become. That faith in people is not based on mere pious hope. It is based upon some real results achieved in the process of cultivating leadership ability in ordinary citizens."

For a people supposedly democratic, Americans have strangely naïve and contradictory ideas about leadership. Most people seem to assume that the ability to be a leader is a rare and much-to-be-admired exception to ordinary experience. In wide belief, the quality is inborn and has a man-of-destiny flavor about it. All this has a tendency to remove the more outstanding of these rare persons from daily human relations with ordinary mortals.

At least two consequences flow from such simple-hearted admiration. In the business field, the "great leader" should be compensated financially far beyond others. In the political field, the "great man" develops a camp of worshipful followers for whom he can do no wrong and a camp of hateful detractors for whom he can do no right. There is no better illustration of this violent contradiction of attitude than in the case of the late President, Franklin Delano Roosevelt. Even after his death there are those who remember his every word and deed as sacred. And there are those who have apparently devoted their lives to a complete besmirching of his memory. Neither camp contributes toward national sanity. These extremes of contradictory attitude indicate a public pathology with regard to one very human leader.

Undue admiration for a leader implies unfortunate subservience in the led. It means that overfaithful followers abdicate their initiative, even, sometimes, in the absence of a specific person to whom allegiance is given. We were called in for consultation by the congregation of a then pastorless church. The organization was dying from inaction. Members faced numerous problems and opportunities which they freely mentioned. We naïvely suggested several possible solutions for their thoughtful consideration, offering our services to help carry out any project they selected.

"We are waiting for leadership," they cried. They meant they were waiting for a pastor to direct and whip up their enthusiasm. We tried to encourage them to believe that leadership ability, like the Kingdom of Heaven, lay within them. But they continued to wait. When, at long last, a pastor did accept a call to this pulpit, it should have surprised no one that he was unable to move the church to action. He resigned in frustration after a year. The congregation had become paralyzed by dependence upon the disembodied idea of a leader.

VARIETIES IN LEADERSHIP

Some of the weaknesses of democracy are to be traced to a confusion of concept about leadership. The word "leader" is used loosely and often with contradictory meanings. The difficulty is one which extends beyond the use of words to include uncertainty as to the kind of person to be followed and the kind of followers he tends to produce.

The Celebrity

Any person who is prominent in some specific field may be referred to as a leader—in sports, in art, in science, in the social whirl. The distinguishing characteristic is ability to catch the public eye or to make the headlines. The ability to attract or command a following is non-important.

The person of prominence is held up for jealous or worshipful admiration. He need not be connected with any group of his fellows. He may live the life of a hermit or possess austere qualities which cause others to reject him as a person. Yet his standing in some admired field of endeavor or his picturesque idiosyncrasies as built up by skillful publicity will allow him to be dubbed "leader."

American naïveté toward celebrities is recognized and exploited by publicity. The endorsement by the prominent of cigarettes or soap is matched by the list of "big names" which must adorn the letterhead of a campaign for almost any worthy purpose. Community organizers-in-a-hurry will often choose an executive committee of "leaders" who command respect, having no intention of calling upon such persons to do any work in an organization. That responsibility is left for lesser folk—lesser, that is, in publicity rating.

We do not condemn the celebrity or the practice which uses him. We merely insist that he is not necessarily a functioning leader. We prefer to save the term for someone who has an interacting relationship with those he seems to lead.

The Expert

Sometimes prominence is based upon a useful skill. A person with specialized knowledge or ability, who may be called in for advice, is often referred to as a leader. Note that he is called in; he comes usually from somewhere else. A man's expertness is frequently determined by the distance he must travel to give advice and by the aura of distance he can maintain while present.

Again, thinking would be clarified if some other word than "leader" could be used for the outsider-with-specialized-knowledge. His suggestions may fall on deaf ears, may be rejected even though valuable, may stultify local initiative. He can be a useful, even a necessary, contributor to community growth. He needs to be called in, used, and interpreted by functioning local leaders who neither reject nor are overawed by the prominence of specialized wisdom. The problem of using the expert without yielding to his domination is always with us. It will be solved only as the confidence which flows from leadership experience becomes more general in the population.

The Father-Substitute

The late Adolf Hitler contributed to modern thought "The Leadership Principle." By this he gave to blind, childlike obedience the blessing of resounding phrase. Though the man himself went down to catastrophic defeat, some of his ideas go marching on in other minds. Possibly the need to follow an all-wise and all-responsible leader was lurking in the thinking of many long before the rise of Hitler and will be present for long after his departure. There are those in any nation who, out of immaturity, or long years of failure, look constantly for a father-substitute on whom they can lay the burden of their indecision.

Probably the native skepticism and raucous irreverence of many an American will help keep the nation from accepting any self-chosen, godlike figure for uncritical obedience. Or possibly a happy plurality of allegiances makes a people avoid centering upon any single person. Those who must follow a fatherlike figure divide themselves among several church denominations, several political persuasions, several corporations and labor unions, each finding a different object of adoration.

Despite such favorable hopes, Americans need to be on their guard lest, in some emergency, they accept a "leadership principle." In any population there are always great numbers of people who tend to make up personal inadequacies by finding some self-aroused leader who "knows all the answers." These folk seek to complete their truncated lives by basking in the certainty and glory provided by an all-wise great man or infallible organization. In the years of constant crisis which lie ahead, the numbers will increase of those who will wearily lay their burdens of despair and confused indecision upon someone who can relieve their responsibility, even though the policies adopted be hard to defend. Even a democracy which seeks to cultivate responsibility in citizens is not immune to such childlike responses.

The "Natural" Leader

Though Americans may be less susceptible than some other peoples to blind followership, there are widely used practices which are more compatible with dictatorship than with the responsibility of democracy. Some of these cluster about the notion and exploitation of "natural" leaders.

If one assumes that leadership is a rare and unique ability, then one readily assumes also that groups strong enough to survive have dominating personalities at the helm. Having assumed the existence of such personalities, one keeps searching for them until found. Having found them, one readily uses them for control of the group.

And one makes little or no attempt to train similar abilities in other members of the group.

It is not too difficult to understand the awe-struck reverence with which the Caesars and Napoleons of history are regarded by some historical interpreters. It is more difficult to realize that something of the same selected-by-fate odor should cling about petty dominators of community organizations. Yet many observers expect to find a personality which has gravitated to the top by "natural" superiority in each street-corner gang, labor union, political machine, women's club, farmers' organization. It is also frequently admitted that this person achieved and holds his position by somewhat doubtful means, by fighting in the gang, by trickery or the passing out of favors in political situations, by appeal to irrelevant emotion which masks true intent. Nonetheless, because of the "naturalness" of this process, such domineering leaders are frequently accepted as inevitable.

We are not denying that strong personalities will often be found controlling the affairs of established organizations. We merely insist that such a condition represents an earlier, less mature stage of development in the democratic process. We do not assume that a "natural" leader must be present, thereby tending to create him. We work with whatever hierarchy of power exists, hoping that the maturity of shared and rotated leadership can be achieved in time.

The Manipulator

Then there is the leader who lays claim to the title by exploiting other leaders. History is filled with tales of fuehrers who operated through sub-fuehrers all down the line of control. But a democratic society, in less mature phase, presents a different phenomenon. This is the manipulator, less obvious but often extremely influential.

The modern public relations expert analyzes his audience to be influenced into groups and subgroups, each with its own interests and point of view. His persuasive appeals are addressed less often to a mythical general public and more often to specific group interest. The task is made easier if there are organizations whose headquarters and officers can be approached. Support for a political position or financial campaign is gained by interpreting the proposed action as serving the needs of farmers, labor, merchants, church members. The manipulator will seek out and gain the support of the "natural" leader of each group, that person whose word of endorsement will (he hopes) sway the decision of thousands.

Here can be found a major reason for the desire to hold a growing democracy at a less mature level by continuing the sway of "natural" leaders. These are useful for exploitation by the professional persuaders who seek to gain support for themselves or their clients.

Most manipulators are content to be leaders behind the scenes, the pullers of strings. They are willing to forgo the plaudits in favor of the power. They may even coyly deny their influence, preferring to allow those they control to take the praise and the blame. The better concealed are these powers-behind-the-façade, the more detrimental to responsible democratic processes. It will be preferable if manipulators have their wish and be referred to as something other than leaders. Their desire to remain relatively unnoticed is another matter. As public relations people, propagandists, political bosses, lobbyists, their power and methods should be open to public inspection.

The Community Organizer

Within the ranks of social welfare workers there have arisen professional community organizers. These people refer to themselves hopefully as leaders. According to the way in which they work, they may become either manipulators or contributors to maturing democracy.

Most community organizers in practice tend to become manipulators. This tendency grows, not out of personal perverseness, but out of the necessity of having to accomplish quick results within a large population subject to much high-pressure demand for attention. They tend to become small-scale operators for compensations a mere fraction of those received by the big-time propagandists. This is justified in many minds by the fact that community organizers are seeking the public good rather than the selfish advantage sought by better-paid persuaders.

Some undoubtedly worthy project is chosen for promotion by the community organizer. This may be a slum-clearing housing project, a series of much-needed parks, or contribution to the annual community chest drive. An organized structure of committees is set up. "Big names" of celebrities are assembled for a façade sponsoring list. In addition to generalized publicity, appeal is made to those separate groups of which a city is composed. "Natural" leaders are used to bring these various groups into line for support. The city-wide organization may in time become permanent, and participating citizens learn to take more responsibility. Ultimately they may even help in the choosing of future projects to be promoted. But the community organizer's attention is concentrated and his job dependent upon his achieving success in promoting the specifically chosen project. The development of stronger citizens for mature democracy is, of necessity, less important and may be forgotten altogether.

Because of the limitations imposed by demand for immediate results, we prefer to abandon the community organizer as a type of leader to be cultivated. When working for results in the lives of citizens, he operates as a community educator.

The Community Educator

Community organizers who concentrate more attention upon human beings than upon the programs they are to be persuaded to adopt are community educators. Teachers willing to step outside the safety of a classroom and learn about the facts of living along with other fumbling adults may belong in the same classification.

The community educator has one supreme advantage over other types of teachers. He has no power over those he teaches; he cannot force them to sit at his feet. They associate with him only so long as they respect his judgment and feel that joint experiences with him are vital. This lack of the power to command gives him opportunity to become a genuine leader as well as a pedagogue. Like that of any other good teacher, his success is measured by the triumph of his students, not by the brilliance of his lectures. He is forced to respect his co-learners, must avoid disciplining them, must offer his suggestions in a manner which makes them more, rather than less, self-confident. Yet this self-confidence must be based upon genuine achievement, not upon the warm vapor of compliment merely. He must be ingenious to help organize and to turn to educational advantage other happenings over which he has had no influence. He must be ready to rescue situations which have lost their direction or degenerated into petty bickering.

There are at least two roles for the community educator as leader: promoter of growth toward responsibility in others and conciliator of differences. These roles are not inconsistent, as will appear later.

But each requires particular skills which can be cultivated. In fact this type of leadership, which triumphs through the achievements of others, requires careful training. It scarcely arises spontaneously through the self-seeking impulses which inspire the usual "natural" leader.

Perhaps the single most difficult understanding to cultivate in the community educator is the willingness to remain in the background or to retire from the scene. The native self-importance of most teachers makes it painful to realize that one succeeds as he works himself out of a job. The end result sought is a strong local leadership, growing out of and closely related to a functioning, democratic group. The community educator is handmaiden to the growth of others.

The Participant-Leader

The idea that leadership represents unique and seldom-found ability has been fostered by those who have already achieved prominence. Such an interpretation is more satisfying to their egos. The belief that leadership can emerge when ordinary people take responsibility for solving their own problems gives new dignity to run-of-the-mine participants. Slavish dependence upon the already successful is no longer necessary. Each person may discover within himself the seeds of unpredictable growth. All this calls for faith in the potentialities and the ultimate decency of ordinary people. It often means a willingness to cling to that faith even when the apparent facts seem to belie it.

One of the reasons those leaders who appear to be "natural" seem so unusual is this: they often present a unique combination of abilities that will be found separately in their followers. Then if we wish to train for leadership, we will break the function apart into different skills and seek to perfect people in one skill at a time.

Too often it is assumed that the major attribute of a successful executive is his ability to give orders, to command. Obviously this is a limited interpretation for people who hope to become more democratic. But it also concentrates attention upon a single supposedly all-important skill. The multiplicity of abilities which are necessary becomes apparent as opportunity for leadership is opened to many people. In a committee planning community improvements these abilities can be broken down into voluntarily accepted job assignments, such as:

Conducting a meeting so as to give free voice to all while making real progress.

Selecting people for assignments that will get jobs done and help the individual to grow.

Keeping useful records.

Promoting interest by public speaking, telephone calls, or "talking up ideas" in the neighborhood.

Obtaining donations of equipment, money, property, or services.

Indulging in physical work, first as participant, then as supervisor of a crew.

Collecting data for a report upon which plans will be based.

Experiment with faith in the potentialities of ordinary people has not been disappointing. Individuals have often developed, almost overnight, outstanding ability in one or more of these enumerated skills. A man will find that he is highly successful in persuading people or business firms to make donations. A woman will discover that she is a builder of confidence in the enterprise. After overcoming the astounded self-admiration of newly discovered ability, the individual is ready to go on to the conquest of new skills. General leadership ability in many people can develop as a result of this piecemeal process.

Perhaps it will seem that the discovery and cultivation of leadership in ordinary people destroy the glamour and thrill that surround those great figures of history who have commanded the loyalty of millions. If so, there is compensation in the strengthening of democratic processes. The leader is no longer remote and removed from followers. He is part of and growing with the group of which he is a part. The leader and led are closer and more readily interchangeable, for both have become stronger together. Decision is democratized, less concentrated in a few. The glamour is lost, but the responsibility is spread. And since more men and women become available who have the confidence which leadership encourages, there is a wider choice in making selection for high political office.

SCHOLARSHIP AND SCIENCE DOWN TO EARTH

Any methods discovered for developing leadership must be subject to scientific discipline. They should be adopted as a result of experiment. Scientific understanding and method need to become more the property of ordinary men and less the exclusive possessions of an initiated few. And men having the potentialities for handling great responsibility should not be overawed either by a mystical science or by its high priests. Scientific method also needs to be democratized.

This means that the wisdom of the scholars should be made more functionally earthy. There is no substantial reason for burying wisdom in inaccessible halls of learning—no reason, that is, beyond the desire of the learned to make of their craft a separate, sacred calling. The most abstruse conclusions of the wise can be stated in a simplified and vigorous form to be understood and used by ordinarily intelligent men. The scientists need additional discipline to make their findings more humanly available. This discipline develops when they meet with the attempt to apply their knowledge to real people facing real problems.

Ordinary men on their way to leadership need to take on new habits. They become more than the receivers, merely, of scientific knowledge. They become participants in the process by which new knowledge is discovered. There is so much to learn in the matter of dealing with our fellow man that the approach must be experimental. The local participant-leader may be guinea pig in the experiment, but he is also experimenter.

Keepers of the sacred fire of science often object to the "loose" use of the word "experiment." It should be reserved, say they, for that strictly controlled situation in which the scientist is proving a single hypothesis without confusion of many possible explanations. When a citizens' committee, after much effort, persuades a city government to adopt and enforce a sanitary ordinance, it is possible to ascribe success to several different causes according to point of view. Similarly, our conclusion that conflict has been markedly reduced by much discussion could be otherwise interpreted. The tryout of philosophic ideas in the confusion of real life is clearly not experiment in the narrow sense. But it is experiment in the sense that all of life is a tryout of that which men believe. To subject the process to scientific objectivity and to thoughtful interpretation is more important than to maintain the semantic purity of a word.

We are rejecting several conventional definitions of science. We do not believe it to be a sacred substitute for authoritarian religion, to be used to pressure men into certain behavior. We do not refer to it as some fearsome power, all the more alarming because misunderstood. We are not limiting it to a painfully exact method, to be used only by those "in the know." We do not believe that in order to become scientific one need be burdened down with a wealth of apparatus, survey forms, schedules, and statistical tables, though any of these may prove useful at times. We refer to science as the method of tested thinking, and therefore available to anyone of normal intelligence who is willing to discipline himself to objectivity. A freedom from prejudgment even on matters close to home and a willingness to experiment with one's own social situation should not be beyond the ability of ordinary men. None of us, not even top-notch scientists, reaches 100 per cent in these admirable virtues. We all can improve with proper encouragement. Training in this attitude and method is part of the picture for local leadership in the modern age.

We work with communities, hoping that local leadership will develop and can be trained even in unlikely looking people. And leadership ability emerges, often to the astonishment of those in whom it emerges. Certain others assume that they are dealing with a rare quality found only in a few "natural" leaders. As a consequence, they find that for which they are looking. There seems to be support for both assumptions and we have proved mainly that human beings tend to respond to those things which are expected of them. If so, then let us expect the best; let us expect those attitudes and behaviors which will make them strongest for a mature democracy. Who knows what abilities may emerge among ordinary men if we treat them more and more as though they were mature!

THE LEADERS ARE HERE

We would conclude that potential leaders are almost everywhere, that they will appear with patience and encouragement, that their ability can be trained remarkably in experience.

When all men are more the masters of their fate, leadership will arise as situations call for it. This seems to be true in the smaller affairs of local communities. We hope it extends to the larger affairs of state, nation, and world. But we do not have evidence to support this wider conclusion as yet. All we can say is that on smaller community scale our assumptions on leadership are proving out.

Where shall we find our leaders? Wherever ordinary human beings work together for the common good.

CHAPTER II

Expanding the Campus

COLLEGES have long justified their existence by insisting that they were training the leaders of the future. Then they limited their own scope by addressing their efforts largely to a selected few "superior" students and by retiring to the ivied sanctity of academic halls.

Would it be possible to redirect the traditional purpose, to adapt it to the demands for leadership of a changing era? Would it be possible to cultivate leadership ability in the citizens of near-by communities, and in the process revitalize the educational process for students?

A college has a unique opportunity to fit into local need. Theoretically at least, the American small college may adapt to local mood, can respond to demand for service, without neglecting those eternal verities beloved of academic teachers.

Such was the belief at Earlham when the Program of Community Dynamics was inaugurated in 1947. A college might make an essential contribution to the civic and cultural growth of a region. But in the process it might also find its own soul, discover its own peculiar usefulness. A so-called Director of Community Dynamics was brought in and given limitless encouragement and a limited budget. Neither the president of the College nor the newly chosen director was quite sure of the possible outcome. They had faith that a vital program would develop as the institution attempted to modify itself to meet community needs.

Earlham is a small college with no ambitions toward gigantism. Its student population of 700 to 750 will probably not be radically changed in the predictable future. It is located in a small city of approximately 40,000 inhabitants in an area of the American Midwest which combines agricultural, industrial, and commercial activities in a usually prosperous balance. Its location provided it with a ready-made social laboratory for the study of intelligently guided democratic growth, if it cared to seize the opportunity. A century-old Quaker tradition encouraged a socially responsible use of the opportunity.

ORGANIZATION

The Program of Community Dynamics was inaugurated as an essential part of a liberal arts education. It was not conceived as field work for the social sciences or primarily as professional training for future community workers. It was therefore set up as an interdepartmental function, using services from every academic discipline represented in the College and stimulating each to make its skills more available to citizen need. The choice of the word "Program" was deliberate. It was hoped to differentiate the activity from "departments" such as history or chemistry and from "divisions" such as social science or humanities.

Basic Purposes

The College is an educational institution with first obligation to students. Anything undertaken had to be justified for its benefit to maturing young people. Do they become better citizens? This was the first and essential purpose.

A secondary and less imperative aim was the revision of the college curriculum. Numerous critics have challenged conventional liberal arts education, and a number of colleges have begun experimentation with changed programs. Most of these have called for a reshuffling of well-accepted subject matter. Would it be possible to revise a curriculum by calling upon a college to step out of the ivory tower and face the real problems of real people? Would not students be well trained as future citizens in such a process? The experience, though at times disturbing, might prove beneficial also for professors.

A third purpose, not inconsistent with either of these, was the development of many better communities through the encouragement of an abler, more self-reliant citizenry. If the College was to learn from contact with communities, was it too much to hope that many towns might be benefited by contact with the College?

A final purpose has been implied but needs to be stated explicitly. This was research. How does leadership develop and work democratically? How far can any one locality go in self-help? How can stimulators and experts be used without loss of local self-reliance?

Classes et Cetera

When the typical professor discovers some subject matter or emphasis which has been neglected, he proposes, "Let us set up a course, or group of courses, to meet this need." Suffering as he does from a self-inflicted course curse, he seldom seeks to achieve his goals through less formally organized means, as by creating a new spirit which might pervade whatever formal arrangements prevail. Community Dynamics at Earlham could not escape the formal organization which would fit it into a registrar's arithmetic, but it could press for the changed spirit.

A Seminar in Community Problems, granting three academic credits per semester, is listed in the College catalogue. Registration is noncompulsory except for majors in social psychology. Students are invited and encouraged to register, or are counseled to do so by their advisers. They are asked to stay with the seminar for a minimum of two semesters in order to have time to participate in the necessarily slow processes of community change. Because the best discussion occurs in small groups, the seminar is broken up into three separate sessions. One stresses human social processes in small urban settings, one in rural, and the third in foreign community laboratories.

These seminars are not classes or courses in the ordinary sense. There are no academic prerequisites except junior standing and that is violated for special interest or unusual ability. Students majoring in the social sciences predominate but those from natural sciences, humanities, and foreign language are urged to take part and are increasing in number. The education is pre-citizenship, not pre-professional; it is intended to be interdepartmental in appeal.

Stress is placed upon enthusiasm and interest. There is no pre-organized syllabus or textbook, but certain basic sociopsychological processes are studied in the midst of participation in real social growth. There are no set assignments or examinations. Rather, students are challenged to take some responsibility for gaining their own education. Their learning grows out of a series of experiences which they themselves help plan. The planning develops in response to needs discovered in community projects. Since students are being trained as future leaders who will encourage and inspire rather than dominate, instructors in the seminars try to work with them in the same spirit.

The seminars are planning organizations for ongoing community programs. Students, both undergraduate and graduate, join with faculty members to determine policy. The seminars agree to accept responsibility in given communities after discussion and agreement by consensus. They analyze needs, difficulties, successes, and failures in order to determine what steps should be taken next. Of necessity, they must appraise the contributions of various personalities in each situation, including themselves and their instructors. Students, when finally convinced that they can express opinions without fear of professorial reprisal, tend to make the most of their opportunities. At first they may spend a disproportionate amount of time in criticizing the sins of their elders, notably the instructors in the seminars. Criticism of those in seeming authority is apparently a necessary stage to be passed on the road to maturity for students. Later they concentrate more and more attention upon constructive responsibility for the success of projects.

The course outline is made cooperatively, mainly on the basis of community need. The seminars block out certain areas of experience and information with which intelligent leaders should be familiar. During the course of a year an attempt will be made to cover all these areas even though community experiences do not always call them up for discussion. Students are usually tolerantly willing to accept recommendations of instructors when they have acquired some of the "know-how" of democratic procedure.

Students registered for the seminars find themselves at the heart of the Program of Community Dynamics. They take part in the selection of projects to be undertaken, in the determination of policy, in the analysis of process, in the disappointment and frustration which are often encountered, and in the quiet triumphs which mark progress. They act as salesmen for other students to register in later semesters. But their influence is felt most sharply when they attempt to explain processes of community growth to "doubting Thomases" among their fellows on campus or seek to recruit volunteers for a variety of service activities.

Often the projects undertaken require more personnel than the seminars afford. During any given semester, the registration will run to a total of from fifty to sixty students in all three seminars. Some job undertaken may require as many as two or three hundred.

A cleanup campaign, a community survey, construction work on homes or public buildings, leadership of clubs or recreation activities—all may call for talent beyond that available in the central seminars. Students operating in collaboration with the Program become promoters of a wide variety of service activities. These are usually engaged in for the joy of service; academic credit is not recommended except for registered members of the seminars. The satisfaction of generosity should be as unblemished as possible by professorial grading.

Special emphasis is given to the work camp as an instrument for organization of altruistic impulse and as an educational experience unmarred by academic compulsion. The seminars may plan a week end of work-study-discussion-recreation and religious experience as a contributory incident in the ongoing development of a community project. Fellow students, who are called upon to pay a small fee to defray costs, are recruited for the experience, together with residents of the neighborhood or town benefited by the activity. Students may thus make a major contribution to an ongoing social process while coming to know the citizens with whom they work most intimately.

The summer work camp has been found a most satisfactory means for participating in community growth in a foreign environment. The international seminar spends part of its time planning for such experience. A group of ten to twenty students, again paying part of their expenses, will spend possibly eight weeks during a summer vacation working with the citizens of some foreign culture on the invitation of local people who are trying to build their collective lives toward higher standards. The experience is universally reported by participants as most satisfying. The weariness and blisters, the mud and the worry are quickly forgotten in the joy of broadened horizons and friendships beyond the narrow confines of home. But even more significant is the fact that work camps can return summer after summer to the same location, thus allowing a long-time study of the process of community growth over a period of years.

These are all educational activities of great significance. Should they be dignified with academic credit?—a question which has been actively debated. So far the faculty has insisted that voluntary service work should be compensated only in the joy of the doing. When, however, service becomes the basis for academic work in seminar or in special study which can be accepted by an academic department as evidence of growth in ability to use a discipline, then credit may be granted. Credit might be allowed for activities such as these: preparation of a series of historical maps showing changes in size of a community; a study of the music of a foreign people; a paper on language idioms in a special locality of another culture; a series of soil tests to lead the way to improvement of agricultural practices. Service should carry its own reward. But students should be encouraged to adapt their book learnings to practical situations.

Outreaches of Influence

Because the Seminars in Community Problems are something of educational oddities, they have effects and influences beyond their own four walls. They have tended to bridge a gap characteristic of American campuses and of American life. This is the chasm between "do-gooders" and practical men of the world. The starry-eyed desire for reform often reaches a high point during college years. This may be resisted by those who regard themselves as practical both in student body and in school administration. The split, however, between frustrated reformers and cynical men of the world can block progress in many a community. Unity is not obtained by taming the one group or by converting the other. It is found in working side by side at real jobs that obviously need doing. When seminar members recruit fellow students for those bigger jobs that require extra effort, they tend to promote unity between antagonistic factions on campus and in community.

The interdepartmental character of the Program and its close relation to community problems tend to make it a disturbing but integrating force on campus. It helps to break down barriers between academic departments by persuading them to work together on common problems. The physical and social sciences have worked side by side in the international seminar to prepare future work campers who are planning to spend a summer in the tropics. Music and foreign language people have worked with sociologists and political scientists. Biologists were stirred to work on problems of sewage disposal and community sanitation. Philosophy and religion instructors have been challenged to apply ideals to practical situations. The list is endless. No educational institution that seeks the calm of well-defined and limited fields of academic study should institute a Program of Community Dynamics.

The Professional Minority

The description of the seminars would be incomplete without mention of graduate assistants. These more mature students are preparing, they hope, for professional careers as community educators. They supervise the seminars and the activities of undergraduates which are there planned. They remain with the Program for two years, receiving a Master of Arts degree in community dynamics at the end of the time. Their academic studies consist of work in social psychology usually supplemented by additional related courses in such fields as philosophy, economics, biology. Each graduate program is "tailor-made" to suit the interests and probable future usefulness of the particular graduate. But the best education comes out of taking responsibility for the confusing worries that are part of a program which deals with vital living. Again it is impossible to escape academic courses. But the most vital part of the education for future professionals comes in the integrating of formal learnings and practical experience that occurs in staff conferences. Graduate students often discover, as young teachers do, that they have not learned something until they try to explain and impart it to students under their supervision. Maturity is achieved in the process of helping others to mature.

The Program in Action

If the orthodoxy of class-course procedure is avoided, some other scheduled activity must take place. The seminars meet at regular hours in the week, like any other course. But to schedule their activities, which are planned to meet community request—that is difficult to reduce to any predictable routine. Students are called upon to find time to carry out the assignments which they have themselves chosen, at times squeezed in between the multitudinous appointments of college undergraduates. Why not schedule regular "laboratory" hours in which to carry out certain tasks in payment for credit granted? Because responsibilities are accepted as a result of community request, frequently at times more convenient to a committee of citizens than to students. To challenge young people with the necessity for finding time for useful service in the midst of other interests is to train them for some of the important decision-making faced by adult citizenship. The great majority of undergraduates exhibit a commendable but realistic enthusiasm in finding the time to complete the tasks which are necessary even though this may seem to burden them occasionally.

During any regular week of the year, seminar students will be found attending meetings with community councils or committees in the evenings or afternoons. They may be setting time aside to help on a survey for half a day, or interviewing key citizens, or drawing up plans for construction and repair of a building, or conducting a recreation program. Week-end periods of labor or even such periods as a Thanksgiving or spring vacation may be utilized, at the voluntary choice of those who are surrendering their time.

During the summer vacation students will leave the campus, and the country, for approximately eight weeks in order to take part in a work camp. This activity entails a double sacrifice—a financial contribution made by each to the expenses of this expedition and the loss of whatever wages might have come from summer employment. Despite the fact that students are called upon to pay for the privilege of working to help others, there are usually more applicants than can be accommodated during any given summer.

Results in the College

Any evaluative statement must be tentative and subject to constant revision. In this type of work, as in many another human endeavor, it is easy to rest upon past laurels and to fail to adapt to changing needs. Further, results would be differently stated by College administration, faculty, supporting constituency, and students.

The administration undertook the Program in the hope that it would prove appealing enough to supporters to be self-financing. This academic gamble has paid in part, and support for the College has come as a result of the activities of this Program. It has become a central point of integration for much of the changing curriculum.

Faculty evaluations range from gentle jealousy at publicity obtained or money spent on such unorthodox practices, to uncertainty, to willingness to investigate, to enthusiastic cooperation. The balance is on the positive end of the scale after several years of operation. The initial doubts were not hostile; they have given place to gradual convincement as opportunities to utilize the skills of various departments have been found.

The supporting constituency seems to have a positive response, at least from those who express themselves. Alumni indicate varying degree of interest, parents are favorable, and the town in which

the College is located seems guardedly favorable. The tension between "town and gown" which is normal to most college-community
relations seems to have lessened after several years. There is still fear
expressed that the College will try to "run the town" and resistance
lest the opposite happen. But this suspicious misunderstanding
seems to have diminished as a result of a number of projects in
which both students and faculty proved useful.

The reaction of the great majority of students is gratifying. Their
enthusiasm carries them into many vigorous activities. Their gradually increasing understanding of processes is climaxed when those
who have been through experiences explain and interpret to the
newcomers. The numbers who voluntarily seek enrollment in the
seminars is growing. Student opposition comes from two types to
be found on any campus. These are the scientific purists who insist
that the Program's experimentation is not scientific enough and the
doctrinaires, either religious or political, who insist that the approach
is too scientific (that is, they believe there is no need to experiment
when they already "know" the answers to problems). These doubting opponents represent a small minority.

Perhaps it was inevitable that a minute but vociferous hard core
of resisters to the Program should develop. These are the students
who insist they must follow a conscience which drives them to direct
methods of forcing people to be "good." Or they are those who will
not subject themselves to the discipline of collective thought and
group decision in the seminars. Students learn by doing, and they
can be allowed to make mistakes on community projects, provided
they take part in the democratic self-control of group thinking,
where proposals that might end our welcome and utility in a community may be examined. Those who reject the discipline in which
they themselves may participate cannot be allowed the luxury of
independent action in a community laboratory, lest their mistakes
end all relationships between community and college. Citizens of the
future must learn the skills of group thinking and decision. Many
resisting students, in time, come to share in the ongoing enterprises.

COMMUNITY RELATIONS

How do we find our way into communities? By being invited to
come. It was not always thus. In our first venture or two there was
need to overcome ignorance of our intentions or suspicion of academic impracticality. After a number of episodes in which students

and faculty fitted usefully into local needs, the invitations tended to increase beyond capacity to meet them adequately. This situation meant that priorities had to be set up for the selection of projects.

A request comes first for some specific service—help on a cleanup, conferring with a planning committee, cooperation on a musical program. We are willing to start with almost any legitimate need, but we anticipate that a growth of interest from narrower to broader planning will occur. The broadening of horizon may develop spontaneously or may be encouraged by the raising of questions on our part as we sit in with policy-making committees. A community project is most successful when it continues to grow from one activity to another, from specific to more inclusive activities, a process of perpetual growth.

Cooperative relationships with communities cover a wide range of intimacy. At one end of the scale is the contact which is almost casual—the supplying of a speaker or two for club programs, the providing of a student team for a week-end cleanup. At the other end of the scale the contact occurs at many points and lasts over the years, we hope. We start with our response to a specific and limited request for help. By increasing the number and variety of contacts, we try to make the relationship more complete. By raising questions in discussion with planning committees or by helping to form coordinating councils when necessary, we try to broaden both community activity and our own understanding of processes of human development.

The priority which determines amount of time to be spent in any community is dependent upon the extent to which we can take part in policy making or planning. Students and faculty members can observe and learn from contacts only as they have a chance to participate in social processes. This is the "pay" for services rendered. Since we make no claim to expertness and since we serve to be helpful, we make no monetary charge. The educational benefit to us is adequate compensation. We give top priority and most time to those communities which seem to teach us most.

Requests for help come from a wide variety of local organizations, churches, service clubs, women's clubs, institutional boards of trustees, planning commissions. If it seems likely that the initial contact will develop into a long-term project, some attempt will be made to broaden the base of interest and support. We hold to the conviction that a program of community improvement should become *the* occasion for healing the wounds between antagonistic groups and for cultivating the not easily acquired skills of cooperation. A coordinating organization, representative of all factions and points of view in a community, may be necessary. Where such an all-inclusive body does not already exist we may feel called upon to help develop one. A general council may be necessary to achieve that "sense of community" which allows a geographical nearness to become neighborliness.

When contact with a community is sufficiently intimate and intensive, a team from the seminar becomes responsible for continuing contacts, study of the situation, and encouragement. A team is usually made up of three to six students supervised by a graduate assistant. These students take on the community as a voluntary assignment, following it through failure and triumph, going to meetings and activities, carrying on research and gathering material as needed. They report progress or its lack to the seminar as a whole, their worries and triumphs serving as inspiration for class discussion and study.

Communities, like human beings, seem to be subject to fluctuations of mood. They are often slow to arouse themselves from lethargy, are alternately resistant to and enthusiastic about new ideas, go through phases of great activity and enthusiasm followed by periods of weariness and rest. Student teams learn to accept these changes. They learn, that is, the hard way. The acquisition of patience is always painful, but more especially so to the young. To curb youthful overeagerness in the face of community quiescence, yet to be enthusiastic when a situation is ready to forge ahead—this calls for a high degree of maturity found in genuine democratic leaders.

We have observed both success and failure, at least according to our critical appraisal. Our point of view often differs sharply from that of people with whom we have worked. At times, we have been convinced that our efforts were futile only to discover that our collaborators were sure that achievements were remarkable. We try to remain calm in the face of triumph *or* setback, knowing that both are incidents in a continuing process. We do not drop a project because of failure. Rather, after attempting vainly to rescue it, we place it under an inactive classification, assign a team elsewhere, and wait for the next upswing of activity. We learn from experience, whether favorable or unfavorable.

Community Evaluation

Without doubt, the objectives of community leaders and our own differ. They wish to solve an immediate problem; we hope to see growth over a long time period, learning about human beings in the process. No wonder there is occasional difference of judgment as to success. The greater wonder is that local citizens remain as tolerant of student inexperience and of academic obtuseness as they do. In a minority of situations we encounter resistance, refusal to allow us to collect information, failure to invite us to meetings, or even actual sharp condemnation. These reactions, we suspect, are due more to our own lack of skill than to any inherent meanness in others. Our responsibility is to turn these negative responses into positive, when they arise. On the whole, however, reaction to our efforts is so grateful and cooperative as to overlook our all too obvious faults.

The Research Task

Anyone working on the problem of community development has a major obligation to keep records of progress, of success and failure. There is so much to learn; there are so few sure answers; and there are people willing to take the responsibility of leadership whenever they can be more sure of how to proceed. Useful research calls for record keeping plus interpretation to indicate the "why" and "how" of events.

Several different types of devices have been used as research instruments to record community progress. None of them is entirely satisfactory. We are constantly searching and experimenting for more adequate methods.

1. The Face Sheet

The face sheet contains basic information about the community with which we are cooperating intensively. It is a useful device to prepare those going out to work on the project. It is not a finished repository of information, but rather a compilation up to date. It is revised from time to time as new or more accurate information becomes available.

2. A Practical History of the Community

Some information bearing upon previous events in the development of the situation is necessary. Such items as founding, various groups which migrated to the section, important personalities of the past, and previous attempts at organization for general improvement need to be covered. This information is often obtained in verbal form from residents. It can be recorded as long as it also is subject to revision with new information.

3. *The Running Narrative*

An acount of all our contacts with the community, the running narrative begins with the first tentative inquiry about our coming in to help and includes all conversations, phone calls, meetings, and work periods. We try to make this an objective description of actual events. In addition to general progress which occurs in connection with our contacts, we attempt to cull out two types of information:

a. Some account of the development of personalities.
   Where is leadership ability discovered?
   How does it develop?
   Can we help to train it?
   This may call ultimately for the making of individual case studies in addition to slanting the running account to make clear how leaders are found and developed.
b. A description of how success and failure arise, how a block to progress is overcome.
   The narrative should be so written as to make it possible to discover how successful are the solutions which we or others suggest.

4. *An Interpretation*

We try to make a clear separation between the objective statement of events found in the narrative and an evaluation in explaining the "why."

So new is participant-observing of human development in action that no finally approved methods have developed. Further, we will not be satisfied until the citizens of communities in which we work are themselves cooperating with us to keep records. We have admitted freely to them that we observe and keep an account, and our cooperators have been most tolerant of our idiosyncrasies on this point. We believe, though, that people should learn to observe and criticize their own growth in order to be conscious participants in the process.

An additional problem sets a limitation upon our research. When a community reaches a period of quiescence, or when our contacts have been reduced to a minimum for a period, the records kept become necessarily incomplete. In all our attempts to stimulate self-help, we regard ourselves as successful when local leadership takes over and the need for our services is reduced to a minimum. Then, how maintain contacts in order to keep records complete? Actually, the progress made when we are least in evidence may be the most significant of all. Some communities, with kindly understanding, continue to welcome us during such periods. Others become understandably indifferent and information recorded must, as a consequence, be sketchy and incomplete.

With all the difficulties attendant upon research in active human processes, we feel that tentative conclusions can be reached, so long as we remember that they *are* tentative. We can begin to describe fluctuations in community activity and responsibility. We can observe progress, suggesting which procedures seem to solve problems, which seem to fail. We can begin to form conclusions about the discovery and training of democratic leaders.

Possibly a most important contribution in the research field lies in the development of self-examining objectivity. We have achieved something here among students. We hope, in time, to achieve more among our collaborators in communities.

THE LABORATORIES

The Earlham Program of Community Dynamics is frankly experimental. The peculiarities of the social situations as well as of the experimenters may well affect the results.

Our domestic community laboratories are located in southeastern Indiana. Whatever virtues or faults are ascribed to midwestern Americans might well be found among the people with whom we have dealt. We try to avoid making any assumptions concerning our collaborators as we begin to work with them. We do not wish to prejudge any situation and are skeptical about broad generalized statements on the peculiarities of men in the mass. Our closest approach to a general large-scale assumption is this: that human reactions have basic similarities despite a wide variety of social traditions; that national, sectional, and even language differences are by comparison superficial. This is not precisely an assumption. We offer it rather as a hypothesis to be proved or disproved.

Urban Centers

The city is a social laboratory of obvious first attention. It is dramatically interesting because of the sharpness of contrast between concentrated poverty and vice on the one side and apparent ease and culture on the other.

There are those who criticize our experience with cities, saying that we have had insufficient contact with huge metropolitan centers. Our conclusions, they therefore hold, cannot be based upon consideration of the really serious problems of modern life. In truth, our intimate city experience has occurred in small centers, with populations no larger than fifty thousand. Contacts with larger accumulations of humanity have been less extensive, more remote.

The scientist almost always seeks a small laboratory situation in which a simple form of a complex problem can be studied closely. The city of limited size often presents the metropolis in microcosm, the chief difference being one of magnitude. There may be conflict between labor and management, between rival religious and social groups. There are slums with their high rate of delinquency, bad housing, and disease. The city must be broken down into districts or neighborhoods for development of adequate democratic responsibility. In a large city there may be a better array of specialized agencies of social welfare. In the small center there is more scope for the amateur to deal with problems of social maladjustment. This in itself makes the latter a better laboratory for study of the social processes by which the citizen learns to solve his problems.

The small city, no less than its bigger brother, faces the problems connected with "fringe areas" and satellite settlements. Bad planning and unregulated vice are to be found in the unincorporated area around the small industrial center. The "bedroom" community to which city-employed workers repair for the night and week end has interested us. There is frequently a lack of local loyalty owing to the pull of the center which provides employment. There is frequently a major indifference to needs for social services and little desire to plan for the general welfare of the place where the worker sleeps and his family lives.

Rural Centers

The rural social laboratory presents perhaps a less dramatic challenge, but it is basically important to study of social progress.

Competent observers point out that rural America is no longer agricultural America. Our experience corroborates this conclusion. Most midwest towns and villages are satellites to larger centers, a considerable portion of their inhabitants leaving home for the day to make their living elsewhere. Others will work in local stores, in repair organizations serving farmers, or in small industries which increasingly are to be found in towns and villages. As the average size of American farms increases, the number of bona fide, full-time farmers decreases. The self-sufficing rural community, made up of picturesque "hayseeds," is a matter for nostalgic yesteryears.

For better than two centuries succeeding generations of American youth have been fleeing the boredom and limited opportunity of supposedly picturesque rural life. The luxurious lure of the great city has now begun to diminish with the technical developments that make country living quite as comfortable. There are opportunities for young people in small towns, opportunities of a type represented by a satisfying life rather than by great wealth or overwhelming power. To rediscover some of the values of rural living in the small communities characteristic of modern life is a major purpose of our work.

We have cooperated with local citizen organizations in communities as diverse as crossroads, county seats, towns around industrial plants, farmer trading centers, and suburban satellites. We have, at times, gone beyond limited settlements to deal with rural dwellers in the open country. From such experience we have concluded that the basic human processes we seek to study are to be observed better in a group of people with a geographic sense of community than in a group held together by a mere common occupation, such as farming.

Foreign Contacts

In the eyes of some critics, conclusions drawn from experience amidst the well-advertised provincialism of the Midwest are significant for that Midwest only. Without seeking to dispute this debatable point, we have sought community laboratories in settings having other social traditions and language. In common with many other colleges, we have encouraged foreign students to attend, welcoming these strangers to our culture in community enterprises as well as in campus activities. But it is our work in community development on foreign soil that gives some broader backing to conclusions on human processes.

Groups of students, under faculty supervision, have worked in other lands at the task of community building during summers. Activities took place on the islands of Cuba, Jamaica, and Puerto Rico in the Caribbean. The immediate task was the building of a community center, school, or recreation canteen in cooperation with local leadership. The ultimate outcome was the study of the reactions of people in a different cultural environment, the opportunity to take part in a process of community development in the midst of a sharply contrasting social setting. Observations and records made during a summer period of intensive work have been supplemented by planning visits and correspondence.

Attention has been concentrated primarily upon rural communities, chiefly because these are the foreign counterparts of our American laboratories. The small town, satellite to a city or with an industry or two, is not often found. Communities are more isolated, self-sufficient, lacking in the amenities of modern life. In some instances both buildings for a center and community solidarity were lacking among families dwelling in a limited area. We have had the experience of being midwives present at the birth of community spirit, the birth being expedited by cooperation between American college students and local folk who came to work together for the first time. The construction of a playground or community building became the means for beginning psychological processes which we had opportunity to observe in continuing growth.

A Campus Without Boundaries

In seeking to expand the learning opportunity beyond the campus, the College had to accept an additional function and responsibility. This was the offering of service to help communities do that which they wished to do. This gave students and faculty a chance to learn while they worked. But since the relationships in the expanded campus are cooperative, the citizens begin to learn also.

CHAPTER III

Discovering Communities

A COLLEGE decides to educate its students by helping to cultivate leadership in near-by communities. What does it look for in seeking a community? A city, a neighborhood of a city, a rural hamlet, a township, a county? Just because a conglomeration of people has a name on the map, is it a community?

The word "community" stirs a response of warm approval in most men, all the warmer because there is wide difference of opinion as to the idea which is being approved. It may refer to some spot of earth where one belongs, or to the emotional glow felt toward friends or to people with common interests, or to such cooperative abstractions as "The Atlantic Community" or "The Community of Nations." Among the experts who study such matters, a community is thought of as a group of people, living out most of their lives in some limited area, with certain major interests and activities in common. But some will insist that only a small place can exhibit true community life, while others will deal with huge metropolitan masses running into the millions. And the question is pertinent: What is the psychological cement that holds men together, that makes them feel that they belong to one spot or to each other?

Such questions are more than theoretical. They must be answered in some fashion whenever anyone seeks to cultivate community life.

COMMUNITY—WHAT IS IT?

We wish that we might give a clear-cut answer to this question, but we cannot. In the final analysis it must be answered by citizens in terms of their loyalty and behavior, not by social scientists with textbooks in hand. But we have to start with some accumulation of people in mind whenever we seek citizen collaborators. We confess to a bias for smaller centers, both because they are near at hand

and because they present a manageable laboratory situation for study of human processes of living together.

Where Do We Work?

Frequently when a college or university develops "field work" opportunities for its students it turns to large cities. The sociologists on the staff are fascinated by the lure of the pathological in delinquency and disease or they welcome the opportunities for placement which established social welfare agencies provide. This preoccupation causes them to overstress the abnormal seamy side of life. Community contacts tend to be limited to the professional social workers and the underprivileged who are benefited by charity. There is little or no opportunity to meet with the citizens who sit on boards or in councils to take responsibility for planning.

Without meaning to condemn the work in large centers, we believe that our opportunities in small-city and rural settings are closer to basic processes of citizen growth. We enter a community, not because there are problems of social pathology to be met, but because citizens becoming aware of their own needs welcome our help. The emphasis is upon the normal rather than the abnormal. The problems met are studied and solved by amateurs rather than by professionals who know all the answers.

In a small community there is a better chance for the otherwise insignificant man, who must remain an amateur, to have a place of recognition, a sense of his own importance. In the great city, thousands may be lost in anonymity. In a democracy it is important that each person belong somewhere, come to function as an integral part of some social organization. Those concerned to promote better community life must work with some group of people small enough to give opportunity for development of the "little man."

A sardonic paradox must be noted at this point. Suppose it to be true that the democracy of community process can be best studied and developed in the small center. Most community "experts" are employed and work in large cities. In concentrating attention upon a social unit small enough to give recognition to "little men" we are mindful of the practical needs of the majority of community organizers who will worry out their lives in the midst of huge populations. We offer no panacea calling for the oppressed of the city to flee their unhappy life in favor of decentralized villages. Nor do we, in imagination, abandon such people to a dismal and crowded fate. We merely concentrate attention upon those situations where experience of belonging together can be intimately cultivated and studied.

What creates a sense of community when this is lacking in some group which lives together? Is it some common disaster such as a flood or epidemic of disease or outburst of gangsterism? Is it fear of some common enemy? All these means are most often found in large cities; they tend to lean toward the negative push of fear or anger. There is a positive pull of cooperation for the good which is to be found primarily in the situation small enough to allow face-to-face contacts.

The publicity campaign as builder of community spirit needs particular comment. Special interest groups appeal to "the community" for support of hospitals, schools, family and youth service agencies—all probably worthy causes. These call for the support of interest, attendance, or, most often, contribution to financial drives. Such campaigns, which seek to stir an otherwise lethargic "public," are largely associated with the necessities of modern city life. With rural dwellers coming to resemble their city cousins, this kind of effort spills over into the country. It is community in a more active, participative, and self-motivated sense that we are seeking in small-center America.

What of Rural and Small-City America?

There is in America a widespread yearning after the small community of yesteryear. This is picturesque, even amusing, and it provides excellent local color for novels, plays, and movies. But it bears little relationship to the facts of contemporary change. The truth is that rural America is becoming rapidly urbanized.

It would be difficult to chart all the changes which are occurring, especially since the processes of reorganization continue at an accelerating pace. Our participative observation of human processes has occurred in a wide variety of small centers. Among these are:

Pre-communities of isolated farmers still using hand tools in so-called underdeveloped areas.

Post-communities of the machine age which have lost their reason for being. They still have the people but have lost the community.

Crossroads settlements and rural villages.

Rural regions, townships, or counties. These often have more than one focus, each of which may prove to be a nucleus for a separate community.

Small cities. These present usually a combination of industrial activity and rural trade. They frequently have to be broken down into neighborhoods in order to find working human units small enough to allow face-to-face interaction.

As a result of active contact with such centers, we have been able to formulate certain tentative conclusions about the changes which are coming to small-town life. A conscious awareness of these factors gives direction to our thinking about community life and its cultivation.

Small-Town Dependence

That traditional prototype of American democracy, the autonomous small town, has all but disappeared. The self-sufficiency of yesteryear, based upon a majority involvement in agriculture, has given place to a majority employment in stores, offices, and factories often in cities remote from dwelling places. Most inhabitants of rural America are becoming a race of commuters. This condition seems to be true of towns in the middle of agricultural areas as well as those clearly satellite to large cities.

Even the farmers, a breed diminishing in numbers, are losing their independence. They become specialists raising skill-demanding products to be sold in distant markets. They are therefore dependent upon those markets and upon merchants who sell needed supplies. They become as much an integral part of a national economic system as do their city-dwelling brethren or their commuting neighbors. The hard-surface all-year highway and car, the radio and television, the chain store and mail-order house all add their contribution to dependence.

Both the unique color and the freedom to make decisions irrespective of outside influence are diminishing. Communities do not exist in a social vacuum; they are parts of a delicately interrelated and interbalanced whole. The development of able local leaders becomes all the more important in an era of interdependence. But the traditional originator of democratic social life, the relatively independent village, peopled with self-sufficient inhabitants, needs replacement in our thinking. Perhaps the more characteristic prototype for our time is the community of commuters, in whom both loyalty to the dwelling place and self-determining leadership must be cultivated.

Power Structures

Small-town America seems to be dominated by traditional powerful minorities. In some instances, the dominator is a single family with wealth and prestige. In others, it is several families having control of a bank, major store, newspaper, locally owned factory, or political organization. In our observation, this appears to be a type of power more reminiscent of an age earlier than the developing era of interdependence. Certain modern developments tend to consolidate the power of traditional ruling families, however. The disappearance of competing newspapers in the smaller centers of America concentrates power so that families of wealth can, if they desire, attempt to control through the single surviving source of news. In one small city dominated by a single family there is a Republican newspaper published on three days of the week and a Democratic paper on alternating days. The Sunday edition is "nonpartisan." All three are published in the same office, produced by the same editorial staff, in harmony with the wishes of the dominant family.

The individuals and families which have enjoyed hegemony are not without their contemporary challengers. The branch factory with offices in a distant city, coming into American small centers in increasing numbers, constitutes one threat. The chain store, the labor union, and the organization of businessmen with policy determined on a national basis are all tending to break down traditional local power structures. The business organization is less feared by families with traditional power than are some other challengers. An easily found common ground of interest makes a peaceful settlement between these rivals relatively easy.

The picture of power in the large city is more confused. Perhaps the mere matter of size makes domination by a traditional few difficult over a period of time. Or perhaps the new rival claimants for power are better organized. As urban ways and urban values invade the country more and more, will labor unions, competing political ideas and organizations come to challenge traditional power? Is the unity of small-town America being threatened by shifts in power structures?

For anyone who would cultivate community solidarity, the problem is more complicated. He is concerned with the fearful inarticulateness of the majority. Whether the fear of speaking up be based upon domination by a traditional few in a small center or upon the more noisy competition of newer pretenders to power in a large city, the ordinary man tends to doubt his own ability to take the initiative. The problem is to plant that seed of self-reliance in him which can grow into leadership.

The Disinherited

Each community seems to have one or more scapegoat minority which is to be "kept in its place" or upon which, if necessary, the frustrations of the more successful can be heaped. The favorite underprivileged folk of America are, of course, the Negroes, although in some sections Orientals, Jews, Mexicans, Puerto Ricans, or other "foreigners" will serve the same purpose.

People are chosen for the role of the disinherited as a group, not as separate individuals. It is preferable, therefore, if some obvious external characteristic makes members of the group readily distinguishable—color of skin, slant of eye or shape of nose, dress, mode of speech, place of abode, kind of religious worship, type of work in which they are allowed to indulge. Contrary to the beliefs of many goodhearted interpreters, there is much more involved than mere racial or religious prejudice. In many parts of the United States people who are of the same race and religion as the dominant condemners, but who are migrants from poverty elsewhere, are among the disinherited. On the west coast sneering reference was for long made to the "Okies and Arkies" (low-income migrants from Oklahoma and Arkansas). In the states just north of the Ohio River the older dwellers in communities are defensive against invading "Kentuckians" (low-income migrants from south of the river).

When we undertake work in a community, we often discover that there is some disinherited group. In one small city we found no obvious nominees for this unhappy role. There was one colored family only, rather well liked. There was no settlement of recent immigrants to this city, no invasion of poorer folk from another state. Shortly we found sneering reference being made to "Islanders." On inquiry, we discovered that the "Islanders" were folk who had lived in a section of the city formerly surrounded by warehouses and railroad yards, a typical slum. This section had long since disappeared and its inhabitants dispersed throughout the city. But they still bore the unsavory title in memory of their or their family's place of origin.

Is there some psychological necessity which calls upon men to elevate their own egos by looking down upon some group supposedly lower than themselves? If so, it is the task of the community educator to encourage a type of research which will tend to eliminate this necessity, to replace the antagonism of frustration with the comradeship of good will.

Overorganization and Overbusy Leaders

In the pre-community of an "underdeveloped" area, there is little organization that pulls people together. They tend to live in isolation. In the small community of nostalgic memory there were a few all-important organizations which served all citizens of a homogeneous population, one or two strong churches, a town meeting, certain universally attended social events. In the small center of the machine age, becoming a post-community, organizations sprout like weeds in an untended garden. And those who are "public spirited" enough to give time to work for worthy purposes find themselves busy almost every night of the week. They complain about being "meetinged to death."

As an exercise in community self-awareness and as a preliminary to the building of solidarity, we have encouraged the taking of an organizational census in several small centers. The legitimate and significant clubs may run into the hundreds in a population of three or four thousand. A single citizen will have multiple memberships and if an important person may hold offices in several organizations simultaneously. Often the proposal to form some kind of coordinating or planning council will be greeted with heavy sighs of disapproval. It may be resisted as rival for both interest and time. To find time on a crowded weekly schedule for meetings will seem next to impossible. Many of the clubs with prior claim on time will be local chapters of national bodies with only secondary local interest. Any integrating effort can run rivalry with fragmenting efforts whose inspiration lies outside the community.

The initial leaders of a renewed community spirit will frequently be found among the overbusy who already carry too many responsibilities. But other potential leaders are there in abundance if they can be found and encouraged. Leisure for dwellers in small-town America is increasing with the introduction of "labor-saving" devices. What becomes of the released time? To discover and cultivate the leadership talents of the hitherto inarticulate constitutes a major challenge to community educators.

Changing Patterns of Community

Nothing is to be gained by attempting to reestablish the early American community of idyllic memory. There are those who believe that social salvation lies in decentralizing our populations to the small centers to recultivate the bucolic virtues. The dream is beautiful, one much enjoyed by city dwellers who yearn for the soil in the abstract and by devotees of a sophisticated "simple life." But it bears little relationship to the probable realities of community life in a civilization that has started down the road of industrialization.

The earlier American small community consisting of farmers who lived off their land and merchants and professionals who lived off the farmers has been too much idealized. But it did have a clear-cut pattern. It did produce a stout and ruggedly independent citizenry. It cultivated and gave scope to a vigorous, opinionated, and often contentious leadership.

The small center of today is changing so rapidly that no pattern can be clearly discerned, not even the form toward which it is tending. Nonetheless there are certain values which can be rescued from the past and used as guide to direct the future. The citizenry have lost much of the fierce individualism owing to specialization, interdependence, and mass production. But they can recapture individual difference in a cooperative situation. There is a change called for in the kind of leaders to be cultivated. Leaders to be admired are less the great debaters of yesteryear and more the humbler folk who can work together. Together they may give a more clear conscious direction to changing patterns of community life (and of democracy) than the eloquent and contentious leaders ever could achieve.

THE REDISCOVERY OF THE INDIVIDUAL

The determination to concentrate attention upon the smaller community is based upon something more than personal preference or stubbornness. The times call out for rediscovery of the importance of the individual citizen. The dictators and the advocates of a police state have made it clear that remarkable social improvements may be had at the price of individual liberty. Nation-wide networks of superhighways can be constructed, whole cities redesigned, even the trains forced to run on time, if men will yield their right of decision to unquestioned authority. A nation which hopes to remain democratic must find other methods for making these and greater achievements. It can do so only if individual citizens are willing to work together for mutual benefit and can learn the difficult skills of cooperation.

In many ways modern American life is antagonistic to the cultivation of stronger, self-directed, cooperative individuals. Among these is the tendency to think of an appeal to humanity in the mass. The advertiser and the public relations expert triumph at the expense of growth toward independent judgment and cooperative initiative. Confronted with difficult problems, citizens will too often seek a solution at the state or national capitol before they have explored the possibilities of local initiative. These are frequently the very people who will later complain about government interference and bureaucracy. Loyalties are developed toward remote organizations, difficult for the individual to control—the industrial enterprise, the labor union, the political party, the great church body. The individual citizen can be assured of his own significance only as he comes to participate in important activities with friends he can see. The individual will be rediscovered in a community unit small enough yet important enough to allow him to function significantly.

Perhaps it might be found that a small group of people living and working together is inherently more democratic than is a huge population. If true, this conclusion would not mean that a large city or even a nation of millions is doomed to mass manipulation. It would mean that large-scale government by and for the people must rest upon the processes and skills learned by individuals in the intimate association of cooperating neighbors. Then the fundamental school for training democratic citizens would be found in those rural towns, small industrial municipalities, or neighborhoods of a great city which develop a sense of unity and responsibility. If we can learn how processes work on small fundamental scale, we can study also how basic social units can be combined into nations, without losing sight of the individual and his development.

The size of community bears upon the question of the kind of leadership to be cultivated. If one tries to work with human beings by the hundred thousand or the million, he tends inevitably to seek out the "big names," the powerful and influential who can sway men in the mass. If attention is concentrated upon the person-to-person process in small groups, leadership ability may be found in humbler and more numerous folk.

We have found that in the small community the participant-leader can be cultivated. Potential ability of this nature is probably widely spread throughout the population. People of ability are not discovered without a determined faith in ordinary men and in the things they can accomplish, with encouragement and training on the job. They can become highly successful local leaders without necessarily aspiring to political office or great social prominence. As a result of such local development of individuals a few future political figures might happily emerge. But our basic interest lies in finding and helping cultivate leadership among ordinary people who must continually solve their own problems. Our experience leads us to believe that local people usually will discover answers to their own difficulties, satisfactory according to the level of understanding which they have reached. Though these may fall short of the perfection sought by "experts," they will both prove adequate and indicate genuine growth toward greater maturity.

COMMUNITY EDUCATION

Though there be great faith in the ability of communities to lift themselves "by their own bootstraps," at times a helping hand may be welcome. Discovery and development of leadership often does not occur spontaneously. Some encouragement by someone may be required. This can be dubbed community education, provided one is willing to conceive of education as something beyond the limitations of the classroom, something closely related to real life.

To many, education is a process by which those who presumably know a great deal tell others, who know much less, what to think and how to act. Contrasted with this is the view that education consists of growth which arises from meeting and solving problems. Community education, according to the first (and more common) definition, occurs when a staff of city planners or top professionals in housing or recreation tell local leaders how to improve conditions. According to the second (and more fundamental) definition, growth occurs when groups study their own problems, possibly consult with experts, but make their own decisions and learn from both successes and failures. Outsiders, whether professionals or amateurs, can join in the process to benefit both themselves and others. But if they come to dominate the discussion, the educational value is diminished or lost. As community educators we have humbly worked with citizens as they sought solutions to their problems, learning from them as they learned from us. As learners we have become convinced that there are no correct or precise answers to the problem of how communities learn to solve their problems. Each situation is different.

There are precise answers to specific questions on traffic or flood control, sewage disposal, or good recreation and education. This is preeminently the place for community service bureaus and planning bodies in universities or in state capitols, or for private foundations. But these organizations, because they are so steeped in their correct information, become impatient with or cannot understand the stumbling and halting by which communities can be helped to educate themselves. A community program in a liberal arts college, because it is free from the burden of expertness, can join in and often expedite the otherwise discouraging process of growth. Because it can be close to local people and local problems it is often consulted long before any experts are called in to offer their superior wisdom. It can often also serve as mediator between expert impatience and citizen misunderstanding.

The great need in community education is to discover how growth takes place. How do people move from indifference and apathy, to awareness that something is wrong, to determination to work for the common good? The professional with his precise answers arrives upon the scene after a most important part of the process is completed, i.e., after the problem has been identified. With a single-minded goal, he may not even become aware of the educational growth occurring after he has been called in. It is this area of process which we have been attempting to explore.

We have no antipathy to experts. They should be called in when needed. Larger communities should employ trained engineers, social workers, executive secretaries when financially able. There is, however, a tendency among Americans to "pass the buck" of responsibility to professionals or to assume that problems cannot be solved because funds are insufficient to employ a top-grade person. In the small communities of this nation much can and should be done by ordinary citizens; jobs can be handled which in larger centers are managed by the paid professionals. The relationship between the ordinary citizen and the expert is one of the as yet unsolved difficulties of democracy. By learning from processes of educational growth in communities, we may be able to offer some suggestions as to how and when the trained person should be used without the surrender to his dominance by the ordinary citizens.

MUTUAL LEARNING

In any good educational process, all parties involved are learners. In community work carried on by a college, learning occurs at several different levels of growth.

Local leaders and citizens	work together to produce a better life for all,	learn from experience and from contact with all the following.
Undergraduate students	prepare themselves to become future community leaders as an avocation,	learn from community contacts, from study, and from analysis of real situations.
Graduate students	prepare themselves to become professional community educators,	learn from the above and from a more systematic study of an emerging profession.
Faculty connected with the Program	seek to discover how human beings work in real life,	learn by observation and recording of events, research in action.
Faculty not directly connected with the Program	help solve problems of real communities but often are not sure how their academic knowledge applies; they	learn by attempting to adapt their specialties to demands of all the above.

All the parties involved in a community development program are instructors as well as learners; they do their best teaching when least conscious of a pedagogical role. When wrestling intelligently with a seemingly unsolvable problem in good company, they learn most rapidly. The growth in the two faculty categories above is often more painful than for the other groups, since professors have often come to regard themselves as luminaries of wisdom needing no instruction from lesser lights.

If college faculty members resist being instructed directly, community leaders are also perverse. In community work we deal with adults who insist upon being treated as adults even though they may at times behave most childishly. This is "adult education" in a broader than customary sense. Most adult education copies the doubtful features of the schoolroom and places grown men and women in a situation to be told, rather than in a situation to learn by experience. As a part of a program of community improvement, an adult school, composed of day or evening classes, might be set up. But the more basic adult education goes on in growth as problems are solved. The fact that no one has specific answers to the unique difficulties of the particular community under study makes the dignity of each adult easy to maintain in a process of mutual learning.

As we enter communities we attempt to maintain two seemingly inconsistent attitudes: first, one of open-eyed, expectant wonder at the unique situations we may find; second, a sophisticated determination to draw the attention of our collaborators to the best accumulated information from all sources. This combination is part of the process of mutual learning. It calls for a willingness to experiment in the light of the best wisdom to date. A small college that is willing to make use of its close contacts with near-by communities can help local people also to achieve this difficult combination of attitudes as it seeks to cultivate the same in students and faculty.

The citizen seeking a better life for his community is and should remain an amateur and learner. If we are to collaborate with him as equals, we must also be amateurs and learners. This status is not just a pose for effect. It must be genuine. Fortunately, the intricacies of each situation are so complicatedly different that no formula from previous experience or textbook will serve. Despite the obvious need for amateurs, we find that we must resist the temptation to act like experts, especially when citizens trustfully turn to us for advice.

The collecting of helpful information for community thinking is relatively easy. There are many "how to" handbooks available. Their adaptation to the problem at hand is more difficult. But the problems of the complicated relationships between man and man, group and group, and the question of how all people may grow together—these need endless study. If we can claim any expert skill, it is in the field of those interpersonal processes which promote community growth and development of leadership ability. But even here, all we can do is clear the way for and expedite processes which are inherent in people working together.

MUTUAL DISCOVERY

The almost universal approval that greets the use of the word "community" may indicate some common denominator of experience. Or it may point to some widely felt yearning for interaction with one's fellows. Is modern man, in losing contact with the earth of a place where he belongs, losing also the satisfying earthiness of useful human association?

Though many citizens may be unsure that they belong to any community, they are often searching for a relationship which is basic to growth of their own personalities. Just what form community will take in an advancing industrial age is still beyond prediction. If we can share with citizens in helping to find the relationship which will complete their lives, we shall be satisfied. We feel that the small center which allows face-to-face recognition of the least of these citizens is the place in which to promote the process of discovery.

CHAPTER IV

Training Participant-Leaders

HOW are democratic leaders trained? By challenge of circumstance? By response of native ability to difficulties? Ordinary unguided social events seem to produce only a few. But processes can be set up to produce more.

The training of leaders in local communities comes as a by-product of cooperative activities for the general good. The responsibility characteristic of leadership is not readily encouraged in classrooms. In a community setting, we do not select a likely looking individual and say, "Now I will educate a leader who will be ready when activities begin." Rather we encourage certain processes to start and then wait hopefully for the situation to produce the person. When discovered, we expect him to grow stronger as the process continues.

Leaders emerge as an integral part of the community project which produced them, yet which they lead. Formal "educational" materials may be used but only reluctantly, preferably on the request of the learner. The ponderous manner of the pedagogue must be avoided. Whoever is guiding the learning process must function as an equal, dealing with equals.

How a Community Awakens

The story of democratic leadership training is the story of community activity for the common good. And the activity comes first.

Many communities are sunk in apathy. This, at least, seems to be the fact to those enthusiastic hopefuls who have struggled to start some improvement activity. A wide variety of reasons for unwillingness to begin anything can be found, such as: "Everyone" is discouraged by some former failure; people will say, "Oh, we tried that ten years ago, and it wouldn't work." Or the situation is split by warring factions which are more eager to score a triumph over rivals than to improve life for everyone. Or people have so lost confidence in themselves that they rely solely upon large political units, the state or federal governments, to solve problems; their participation consists only in sending a delegation to lobby in the capitol, or to complain. Or they may be so wrapped up in the affairs of their own business, or family, or church that they cannot be bothered with the general welfare. Or they may be just indifferent, unresponsive.

Any of the above "reasons" may be offered as "alibi" explanation for failure to undertake needed improvements. Frequently several of these are found in the same community, combined with several others not mentioned. Perhaps, in the face of all these, people are sitting around waiting for some "big" person to come along, one who knows what to do. If so, the problem is to persuade folks to cease looking for a "Messiah" and go to work.

It is hard to generalize on how apathy should be overcome. Each case is different. Perhaps a process can be generalized by examination of one specific community project. By not too strange coincidence, the story gives a description of one of our most successful efforts.

The community in question is a neighborhood of a small city. The population of the section is four to five thousand, out of a city of approximately forty thousand. Natural boundaries, a railroad line complete with freight yards, factories, and warehouses and a not-too-inviting river valley separate the section from critical neighbors. These latter will tell you that inhabitants of the area are inferior socially, financially, and in geographic location. In fact, before any activity began, we were assured that any attempt to stir local responsibility was foredoomed to failure. Had these people been capable of self-help, we were told, they would have taken steps to improve their condition long before we began asking questions.

Perhaps the predictions of failure intrigued our amateur interest. Or perhaps the fact that the neighborhood population was made up of Negroes and whites with mixtures of new immigrants presented some unique factional confusion to challenge the "do-gooder" in us. Or perhaps the existence of demonstrable need seemed to make for an obvious beginning. In any case the social laboratory chosen was small enough to allow for development of face-to-face democratic functioning. Natural barriers made for geographic unity. Whether there was a psychological sense of community identity or pride was doubtful.

A common first step in awakening from apathy is the development of concern about some problem on the part of some local person or group. The presence of a problem does not start the process. That may be years or decades old. And the longer an unsolved difficulty has become a worry which people accept as an unhappy part of their lives, the more difficult it is to stir action in solution. The process begins rather with the awakened hope that something can be done.

Help from Outsiders

In this instance, there was no initial local stirring of interest. Our attention was first drawn to the neighborhood by the city engineer, not a resident of the area. The next contact was with the principal of the elementary school, also a "foreigner," but a man universally respected and trusted. He was eager for local leadership to develop but felt that a nonresident schoolman should not stand out too prominently. But he was willing to bend every effort to help awaken indigenous interest. There were many needs which non-residents could see. Were local people conscious of these also? To all outward appearances residents of the neighborhood shared the conviction that initiative and ability were lacking in themselves.

In consultation with the school principal, we agreed to attempt the awakening of hope in a seemingly hopeless situation. He believed that the possibility of organizing better recreation facilities for children might stir a response. As bait, the willingness of college students to cooperate could be offered. We set a date for a meeting to be called at the school. Students went to work to drum up interest, looking toward formation of a neighborhood council.

In a self-contained small community, usually it is wise to seek representation of all significant organizations. That is, contact must be made with all service clubs, churches, business organizations, labor unions, women's clubs, and so on. In dealing with a fragment of a city, we discovered to our dismay that individuals were often members of city-wide organizations, which had no specific interest in the neighborhood. Many were unaffiliated. There were a dozen small churches, but numerous folk had membership elsewhere. The nearest approach to a group identified with the neighborhood was the Parents' Club of the school. This was a mothers' affair with no representation of the childless and with a seldom-attending male auxiliary. Such a poorly representative group was the best prospect for a beginning.

The Parents' Club agreed to sponsor a public meeting to talk about local recreation needs. Their children distributed mimeographed announcements from house to house. The city's one newspaper carried announcements. Result? Three residents of the neighborhood appeared at the "public meeting." Several students went home reluctantly lest the gathering appear to be a misplaced class of the College rather than a community meeting. Bravely hiding discouragement, we hope, the principal and those from the College talked about certain possibilities for self-initiated improvement of recreation, called upon largely silent citizens for their ideas, and set a date for a later meeting.

Stirring Interest

One constructive thing was accomplished by the first group of three who came together. They drew up a list of all neighborhood churches and agreed to persuade their pastors to invite students to address them about the proposed council and its possibilities of accomplishment. These promises were carried out and the invitations were extended. Thus local people began to assume some responsibility, even though they yet leaned upon outsiders to make the speeches. All churches were visited by students before the next meeting, with responses ranging from cordiality to indifference.

The second meeting was a little more hopeful. Five attended. Over a preliminary period of approximately three months, with people coming together usually every two weeks, the attendance never rose above ten, despite the best effort to "talk things up" and continual circulation of announcements. Best results came from printed circulars distributed by school pupils, the cost of which was met by donations from the pockets of a few of the faithful. We were forced to conclude that these people did not readily meet to discuss. We discovered later that they would turn out, fifty to two hundred at a time, to work.

Forming a Council

As a result of continuing conversations, certain faithful folk began to emerge as personalities with interest and ideas. These were potential leaders. Up to this point, meetings had been called and conducted by an instructor from the College. After some three months it became apparent that the time for transfer of responsibility had begun to arrive. The faithful-with-ideas agreed that this was true and helped to plan a mass meeting, at which time a permanent neighborhood council could be formed. Temporary committees set up the arrangements and prepared a slate of officers. The great night finally arrived after as much promotion as the faithful could muster. The "mass meeting" was held in the school gymnasium with thirty-six people present. The press, whose cooperation had been solicited in advance, was on hand, took pictures, and loyally wrote a favorable story. The community council, consisting initially of ten people, was launched. There were both men and women on it, both Negro and white. With official organization completed, we outsiders could retire to a role of advisers only. Local leaders then began their process of training through experience.

The fact of small numbers in attendance at meetings should never discourage those who seek to develop local responsibility. Enthusiasm in a handful is of greater value than passing attention from the many. Better six who are determined than sixty who "go along." The process of developing participant-leaders starts with the few who will work; and there is no vital learning without vigor. Other leaders will emerge and be trained by participation in the activities which the first few inaugurate.

In the election of officers, we raised the question as to whether the meeting wished them to be divided evenly between the two races. This was strongly rejected by several speakers. The burden of their argument was this: "We have a job to do to get better recreation for our kids. Let's choose those who will get the job done best. We don't care whether they are white or colored." Success was foreshadowed by determination to avoid an irrelevance.

The First Project

A community council is not just formed. It is formed to do something. At first it may have a general purpose. But it never moves toward vital experience until this is sharpened down to a first active project.

There were (and still are) glorious possibilities before this council—a neighborhood park, a building for a recreation center. But the first task they accepted for themselves was development of a playground for the immediate summer. They had no money, no property, only the enthusiasm of determination.

The catalogue of council achievements on the first project is long. They located a vacant piece of property, large enough for a playground. They persuaded its owner to postpone plans to build on this and donate its use for recreation purposes. They organized several work periods for their neighbors to help them clear out weeds and tin cans and to fill in hollows. They obtained donation of the use of a bulldozer to level part of the field. They laid out baseball diamonds, horeshoe pits, volleyball courts, a stone fireplace for picnics. But they insisted that supervisor of activities was a professional job, for which adequate pay was necessary. They persuaded the city community chest, therefore, to appropriate sufficient funds to employ two playground supervisors and to purchase certain basic equipment. The influence of the College helped quietly with the community chest. In subsequent years, the council has taken full responsibility for obtaining help from community chest. It raises further money to supplement this aid.

That first summer a successful playground was conducted. Neighborhood residents from toddlers to old men and women were served. The Negroes were in majority at first. But as time went on and people became more accustomed to the idea of two races playing and working together the proportion of whites gradually increased. Several special family days were held to clean up the grounds or just for good fellowship. A small amount of money was raised by shows, and by rummage and bake sales, in order to defray expenses beyond contributions from the community chest. Throughout the summer, members of the council and those they brought with them spent as much time on the grounds as possible, taking pride in their joint achievement.

Question has been raised as to why this council succeeded so well with its first project. We learned later, from his own confession, that a prominent member of the city common council had openly predicted failure. He said, according to his own story, "If the College people succeed in striking even a spark of response in that neighborhood, it will be a miracle." Then, a year later, he gleefully added, "They didn't strike a spark. They started a bonfire." This view would give all credit to us. The opposite view was that we had ignited an explosion which was all ready to go off. Neither extreme view seems adequate. From this and other experience, we conclude that ability to cooperate in thinking through important problems is potentially present in most communities, and that leadership will appear and be trained as progress is made. Certain communities may be ripe for action despite discouraging beginnings. Others may be unready despite some brave talk. We know as yet of no sure way to judge readiness except by a tryout.

The Emerging of Leaders

Those who went through the discouragement of poor response and poorer attendance at meetings became aware that things did not begin to move until a leader appeared. He came in the form of a man whose qualifications rested more upon determination to solve a problem than previous leadership training or experience. He had been a member of organizations before, but never an officer. His vigor made him the obvious choice for chairman and he learned many of the necessary skills on the job. Others appeared as well. One man gained the respect upon which much leadership is based by his ability to work hard. Another, a Negro, surprised himself by discovering that he possessed a peculiar talent in persuading merchants to make donations for picnic prizes or sales. Another inspired trust by keeping unassailable books of expenditures. All grew immensely in stature by developing an ability to talk in meeting, to disagree without rancor, to arrive at sufficient understanding for action.

Certain leaders have remained throughout the life of the council. The chairman has continued, though he insists each year upon an election to afford the opportunity to choose someone else. He has become a skilled encourager of discussion and summarizer for action. Some others have remained with him; some have rotated in and out. A successor to the chairman is being groomed to replace him lest the council become too dependent upon one individual.

How a Community Stays Awake

A community awakens from apathy when a few of its citizens discover a ray of hope that problems can be solved. In the process they become leaders even though this be new experience for them. They succeed if their determination to solve a problem looms larger than loyalty to factionalism.

The Slump

The end of the summer brought the first project to a clear-cut end. The members of the council had worked hard, after hours of paid employment and on week ends. The cessation of responsibility was welcomed with self-congratulatory relief. They were apparently conscious of a job well done beyond their greatest hopes. But they wished now to rest. As a consequence, the council became inactive for a period of three months. It came to life long enough to conduct a Christmas party for young people in the school, then went dormant again until preparations for the second summer's playground challenged interest once more.

A slump in enthusiasm after the first success seems to be characteristic of most community councils. Often it is not a response to failure but to success. Similar periods of slowdown are interspersed between episodes of lively activity throughout the life of such volunteer organizations. As in this case, such periods do not necessarily imply permanent lack of interest or the possibility that growth has ceased.

Overeager promoters of community activity may become impatient or alarmed during slack periods. As a consequence they redouble the pressure to get something done. This is a mistake growing out of misunderstanding of educational processes. Maturity in people cannot be coerced. Forced learning is impermanent learning. Or it is learning that produces resentments which cause rejection of the hoped-for new habits.

During a period of slump a community leader-in-training is exercising his right to be human. Growth is seldom a smooth, even process; it occurs by irregular fits and starts. It is unwise to attempt to force a council or leaders into activity for which there is no readiness, or during a period of quiescent digestion of changes which have already taken place. Communities, like individuals, fluctuate through phases of rest and wakefulness.

The uneven character of progress in human growth is particularly noticeable when activity is voluntary. When the threat of poor grades in school or the whip of pay in employment make for coerced learning, the alternating stages of rapid progress and of lying fallow tend to be masked. The leadership learnings taking place in a community council are based upon willingness to work and learn. This willingness should never be violated.

As the second summer approached, the neighborhood council awoke to new life in time to prepare the playground for a new season. The awakening occurred not by reason of our skillfully phrased (we hope) questions but as a result of pressure from a problem for which they were willing to accept responsibility. The return to activity was at a higher level than were the previous efforts. The council was prepared to avoid earlier mistakes. New equipment could be added to that already on hand. But most of all, responsibility for money raising could be increased through functions on the playground. A small building to house equipment and a soft-drink counter were begun with both local and student labor.

Expansion of Interest

Then began a process which has been observed in numerous settings. A community council, having awakened people, stays awake by moving on to new responsibilities. The new phase may be the initial project at a more elaborate level. But best is activity calling for expanding skills and challenging as-yet-untried energies.

The new interest was cooperative building activity. Council members, citizens of the neighborhood, and students had worked together on construction of playground facilities and a small building. Many neighbors were obviously in need of repairs to run-down homes. Cooperative work to help the most needy seemed a logical next step. The council and its leaders undertook to operate week-end voluntary work camps to improve private homes with the aid of occupants. The council determined priority on jobs to be done, recruited volunteers, assembled tools, and helped beneficiaries with purchase of materials such as nails, lumber, and paint. Their major triumph beyond the building on the playground was the construction of a complete small house for a family which had previously lived in an abandoned bus body.

The council continued active, having conducted playgrounds for four seasons. It was undismayed by the threat that the property which has been used may be reclaimed by its owner as a site for apartment houses. Leaders negotiated with this owner, but developed plans for using another piece of property when their efforts with him failed. They talked confidently of being able to raise enough money to purchase land to be donated to the city as a park or to a social agency. (Four years earlier they registered horror at the suggestion that they should raise money.) They continue with voluntary cooperative construction activities in the neighborhood. A late phase was an interest in a more ambitious program of self-help house building. They studied federal housing legislation and the legal-financial phases of such a cooperative operation. These are all plans in the making. There should always be new activity under contemplation and study in order to keep a council awake.

Other possibilities lie before the council which may point it toward new functions. The social agency which had cooperated over the years to administer funds solicited from the community chest purchased a property in the neighborhood. It proposed to develop an interracial social center to service the section in which the council had been working. Would the council be willing to join forces in this endeavor? Council members were willing provided they could maintain their identity as a group; provided also they of the neighborhood could have a strong voice in policy making. Several members of the council were taken on the board of trustees of the agency, thus giving it more of a local color, close to the people served. The council is in process of becoming an amateur citizen auxiliary. It will have a headquarters but will maintain its own independence. And it will be at the planning center for improvement of the entire neighborhood. Perhaps the council and its members will grow by changing functions to meet new opportunity.

The Incompleteness of Progress

No apology need be offered for the indeterminate state of the council when last seen. If it had died it could be described as complete, a finished thing. Instead it is alive and changing, as are its members. Progress is always incomplete.

SCHOOL FOR LEADERSHIP

The training of participant-leaders is a long process. It is never completed, for the capacity for human growth is unlimited. One of the reasons community organizers-in-a-hurry have assumed that leadership ability is so rare lies in a weary unwillingness to continue training over a period of years. A council serves as an awakener of a community with a continuing series of projects. An energetic community council is an ideal school for democratic leadership.

Self-Confidence, a Measure of Maturity

An observer who was present at earlier meetings of the council, then at meetings late in its career, would be impressed by one clear-cut change—an increase in the confident manner of the members. Though this is a subtle thing, difficult to measure accurately, it is real. Investigators of social processes can describe a difference in the

prevailing spirit of a group which allows some prediction of probable success or failure. The amount of confidence exhibited in a
council is a surer gauge of growing maturity than is the number of
successful projects.

By the end of the third year, members of the council discussed a
variety of topics with assurance. They had met and conquered a
sufficient number of difficult situations to be sure that they could
handle new challenges. They had met and overcome such worrisome
problems as finance, employment of supervisors, repair of equipment, mobilization of community sentiment and people, obtaining
of donations, promotion and carrying out of programs in schools and
on playground, obtaining favorable publicity, keeping good relations with city officials and public welfare agencies. When someone
is asked to take responsibility for an assignment, he tends to accept
the task with the calm confidence that he will be able to carry it to
success. This attitude stands in sharp contrast with the coyness and
hesitancy which appeared in the early days. Suggestions for new
enterprises are likely to be examined on their merit, rather than
rejected out of timidity. Clearest indication of all, the council
members no longer lean upon people from the College who had the
patience to wait for leadership ability to emerge. They can and do
operate without us, though they politely invite us to attend meetings and are willing to give critical examination to suggestions from
us. They live the role of responsible citizens solving their own
problems.

Growth toward mature responsibility occurred quietly, apparently
without their consciousness that they were engaged in a learning
process. To all appearances they were aware of problems solved,
not of personal change. There were spontaneous expressions of
satisfaction with achievement: "Well, that's finished," "It wasn't
so hard after all," and the like. At length there was reminiscing
about things done which originally seemed beyond their powers.
There has been mention of parliamentary skill or the use of humor
to smooth out tense situations which they observed first in us, then
adopted for their own. Special spontaneous mention has been given
to change in attitude on race. Individuals at first had practically
no dealings with citizens of the other race. They worked with the
others either hesitantly or with self-congratulations for liberalism.
Finally, they accepted the others as friends with motives and abilities

similar to their own. Consciousness of growth came as a reminiscent summary after the event.

Recruitment Through Rotation

A community council acts also as a school for leadership by rotation of personalities into and out of responsibility. Much more is involved than an annual election of officers. There is constant recruitment of new potential leaders to be trained by the acceptance of responsibility.

A council when active has many jobs to be done. Members normally seek out their friends and neighbors to help, whether the task be physical construction or the deliberations of a committee. Those who show special interest or aptitude are asked to serve permanently and eventually are invited to become members of the council. The fact that new faces appear and some others disappear as time goes on need alarm no one. When many activities are under way, there is room for large numbers of people who are ready to begin growth toward leadership.

Doubters and Critics

The continual search for potential leaders is the best answer to the problem of the "holdout." When a community council is formed, there will almost always be some refusal to cooperate. Even in the case of a council destined for great success a few doubting people or organizations will be found. This small group of "holdouts," who will not participate in the organization at the outset, can often be enlisted gradually by involvement in committee work and other activity.

A determined doubter cannot be won over by answering his doubts. He is won over by involvement in action. Frequently the objections expressed cover a wide gamut from the irrational to the fantastic. Some of the oppositions expressed to the work of the neighborhood council were:

We people cannot do anything to help ourselves. We must have the help of the "big bugs."

The idea is "crackpot" because it calls for a mixing of races.

No church should support a recreation program. The job of the church is to deal with spiritual life.

I'm too busy to be bothered.

We poor people do not have enough money to do anything.

There is no adequate answer to such doubts, no answer but for those who have the convictions, on which leadership is based, to move ahead. The shortsightedness of the doubt was demonstrated by the success of the council. Doubters were gradually won over by work rather than by argument. They became involved in activities which interested their friends and neighbors. It is often found that people who refuse to take part in the general planning will work on specific jobs. They make progress toward leadership ability as they work their way from specific jobs to general planning.

One characteristic which newly developing leaders must acquire is the confidence to keep working in the midst of criticism. There will always be complainers and critics against any program of action. Sometimes the chorus of objection rises to such a crescendo of sour notes that harmony for achievement is destroyed. Then considerable time must be spent in talking out the difficulties and in reassuring the doubters. Sometimes the complaints are no more than the nagging of an unconvinced small minority and the doubts of potential leaders who have not yet learned to think in terms of the welfare of all. For these the best answer is twofold: Let doubts be freely expressed; answer them by proceeding in quiet confidence to do the job. The leaders of the neighborhood council wisely gave the answer of quiet achievement rather than that of argument. When inevitable complaints arise, the reply of deeds is always appropriate. A supplementary discussion or explanation is sometimes necessary. To know when to add the verbal extra is one of the skills in judgment which can be learned only in experience.

Amateur Standing

A community council is a school for democratic leadership, not a training institute for politicians. It is successful when it raises the general level of responsible competence. It must maintain a status as amateur, free from commitment to political party, established government, church denomination, or other body beyond local control. It should never solidify into an institution with a well-equipped office, a large budget, and an employed permanent staff. It is not a substitute for or a rival of established agencies, governmental or quasi-governmental. It should be an organization of amateurs, expressing the too often inarticulate voice of the citizen.

The neighborhood council remains, as it should, an unofficial organization of amateurs. Its members raise small amounts of money for incidental purchases of equipment on the playground. When it comes to large expenditures, they enlist the interest of the established social agency which then handles the funds. They appeal to the city government for certain actions supplementing their own efforts. They *do* pay for insurance on playground equipment and supervisors, lest someone mistake them for men of wealth and power. If and when they enter the self-help housing field on large scale, they plan to encourage formation of a separate corporation to handle complicated problems. The council should continue to be an informal, freely discussing and freely recommending body with influence no greater than the persuasiveness of its members.

Amateur standing can be maintained either by exclusion or by inclusion of all factional fractions of the population. The neighborhood council chose the method of exclusion, both because its scope was less than city-wide and because inexperienced leaders were less likely to be able to cope with the vociferous confidence of those already established. The long-time respect accorded a council is dependent upon its genuinely representing the general public interest, rather than some self-seeking minority. In the long pull this purpose is best achieved by including all factions and interests. The method which seeks to include all requires or creates stronger leaders.

Governmental agencies are only part of the story of mature democracy. Too often Americans have entertained the notion that democratic growth could be achieved only by electing better public officials. Though enlightened administration of constitutional authority be important, it needs supplementation by amateurs devoted to public interest. Even the quasi-governmental organization, such as a community chest or privately supported welfare agency, frequently falls short of giving critical voice to the ordinary citizen. The official institution, with power of decision and coercion, with control over a budget and equipment, with buildings and a staff of employees at its disposal, should be paralleled by organizations speaking for citizen interest. The community council, jealous for its nonofficial amateur standing, is a prime example of a parallel function. It can stir officials to action, can seek to pass on its ideas to agencies better prepared to carry them out. Its main task is to raise the level of leadership responsibility among the citizens of an active democracy.

The Achievement of Greatness

We are not assuming that the experiences of a neighborhood council in a single small city set the type for all community endeavor. We have offered them merely as a basis for discussion. Each situation is peculiar to itself; each is unpredictable as compared with previous experience. It is this very variety and unpredictability that make community growth so fascinating, that open the way for infinite possibility in development of the personalities of leaders.

In a small way the leaders who found themselves in this neighborhood and in dozens of other community enterprises achieved a minor greatness. They stretched their stature beyond the point which they had thought possible. Theirs is the simpler greatness of accomplishment for the common good, in answer to need which they themselves have discovered. Perhaps this is a more significant achievement than is that which receives loud acclaim. Perhaps these folk risen to humble leadership could stretch their stature further to assume responsibility for high policy, if the situation should offer sufficient challenge.

Growth in many communities leads us to conclude that greatness, defined humbly, is potential in most men. It appears with a challenge that holds out a hope. It grows with achievement in the solution of problems that affect the common good.

Glamorous greatness exhibited by the single, isolated individual is good for exciting publicity but is limited in social value. Greatness based upon ability to work with others cooperatively is even better. It is more in keeping with the needs of an age which demands maturity. Those who have achieved such greatness report that the process was exhilarating. It was also painful. Significant growth always is.

CHAPTER V

Training Future Citizens

CITIZENSHIP training for the young has long been a legitimate concern of American schoolmen. Traditional activities in this field have been suffering critical reexamination. Believers in democracy have been alarmed to learn how easily educational processes could be prostituted to develop slavish citizens for dictatorship. It should be clear that education for future citizens of a democracy cannot be left to the casual school practices of the past. Such training must be vital in order to meet the challenge of indoctrination by the dictators.

One painful fact needs incessant repetition in the competition between free societies and dictatorships. To teach young people to be subservient to authority is relatively easy. To teach them to achieve the maturity of self-directed responsibility is much more difficult. The creation of slaves is easy. You simply give orders backed by threat of torture, concentration camp, or death. The development of free men requires more intelligence, more patience, more faith in human beings. No one can be forced to be free. Men can only be invited and encouraged to accept the responsibility of freedom.

Much of traditional American citizenship education lacks a vigor sufficient to compete with the artificial excitement and leader-chosen security of dictatorship. It is too bookish, too academic, too centered in a curriculum preselected by authority. This statement has been true of courses in civics and history, of memorization of great speeches and the legal documents of constitutional government. None of this has involved the student in the functions and hopes of citizenship: he did not have any experience of working for the common good. He spent time in absorbing words, not in learning how to take responsibility.

In training future citizens in a college, we have sought to base the learning upon vital experience. We have plunged undergraduates into the process of community improvement as carried on by active men and women, who themselves are learning to become better citizens. We do not cast aside the books and the academic helps; we merely take them up in connection with the needs of real experience. The whole process, real life supplemented by reference books, is digested in discussion.

We have been asked: "Do you dare to turn loose inexperienced and naïve college undergraduates to mess around with the complications of community development?" The answer is a direct, "Yes," but under a self-accepted discipline of responsible group discussion. As far as we can see, working at real problems in communities has done no more injury to those communities than some professionals could have done. We dare because we have faith in the ability of young people to assume the responsibility that is necessary for successful democracy. Our community collaborators have usually accepted the same faith.

Educators who would seek a vital citizenship training for youth need to divest themselves of a characteristic bit of elderly arrogance. This is the conviction that they know enough about good citizenship to instruct the young. Commencement speakers by the score assure bright-faced young people that they must do a better job than bungling elders have done—after teachers have made a four-year attempt to shape the young into replicas of those same elders. Actually, it would be difficult to obtain any widespread agreement upon any traditional pattern in which future citizens should be molded. Agreement upon any new fixed pattern would be even harder to obtain. The best citizenship training is that which lays stress, not upon any predetermined blueprint of behavior, but upon the processes by which citizens grow in responsibility. The young begin to develop responsibility by helping to select the pattern toward which they should grow.

Especially inappropriate for citizenship education is that extreme expression of elderly arrogance known as the grading system. It is possible to give marks from excellent to failure on matters of academic accumulation of knowledge, but not on the subtle skills and infinite variety which make for citizenship among free men. Unfortunately the ability to please teachers is not coterminous with ability to work democratically with one's fellows. We have therefore sought to evaluate progress by another method: interest as evidenced by willingness to volunteer for responsible jobs-to-be-done.

A CURRICULUM OF ACTIVITY

There is no satisfactory textbook for education of future citizens, no set outline or curriculum. Experiences must provide opportunity for learning. How are experiences chosen? More requests for student help than can be met come from communities—an evidence that we are not too unwise in daring to trust students to make themselves acceptable. "How do you choose the most suitable activity?" we have been asked. We give top priority to those invitations which promise to bring students closest to policy making and planning responsibility. There is always plenty of drudgery and boresome "leg work" in any project pointed toward general improvement. Many communities are willing to make use of student muscle and enthusiasm. But first consideration is given to those projects which allow an opportunity to observe and discuss the "why" of the hard work.

Almost any activity into which citizens enter with public-spirited vigor, when opened to youthful participation, becomes an unregimented classroom for citizenship training. A few typical activities will illustrate how real community experiences have become the basis for a curriculum of citizenship.

Recreation

Requests for help in developing or maintaining recreation activities for young people are so frequent as to seem almost universal. Perhaps this situation reflects the bafflement that modern elders feel at the unpredictable antics of their offspring. In some cases the job calls for the setting up of a teen-age canteen or a recreation center in a church or school. The need for a playground may be great. Swimming pools and public parks are insufficient in most American towns. The promotional work, the construction, and the supervision afford opportunity for students and adult citizens to learn together.

It is easy for promoters of recreation to make this activity into a self-justifying end. There is a frequent general assumption that the attempt to provide a happy time for young people is always good, that it reduces delinquency and makes for better growth to adulthood. The same prescription is thought to be equally good for grown-ups. The doubt which can easily surround such assumptions calls for the active discussion of recreation activities by planning committees, including the benefited young people. The experience of providing a good time for people is pleasant. But recreation can be superficial or even harmful unless it fits into a general plan of community improvement.

Adult Education Activities

Adult education may cover such a wide range of diversity as a community chorus, a square-dance group, or a public forum for discussion of controversial issues. We have found that adults will accept the suggestions of college students on such matters as long as they come from fellow learners rather than from would-be teachers. Mature adults seem willing to discuss their own learning with young people as long as the youngsters do not "know it all."

Health and Sanitation

In this country, maintenance of health is a matter jealously guarded by trained professionals. Nonetheless, there are numerous activities in which the energy of young people will be welcomed even by the professionals. A town cleanup is needed at least once a year in most American communities. A project calling for the construction of sanitary privies in a rural area or a campaign for cleanliness in a city is possible. In these matters students can work as forces auxiliary to, but in friendly consultation with, authority. Health specialists, in common with other experts, can learn much of the art of democratic functioning by working with learning students.

City Planning

To some it may seem that the complications of modern planning call for the best-trained and most mature minds of any community. We agree—with a proviso. In a democratic society, public planning should be made democratic. The experts on sewage disposal, park development, and housing must be consulted, to be sure. But policy must be adopted by nonexpert representatives of the public interest. We have found that students can carry much of the burden of surveys to gather needed basic data. We have found further that their often halting and incomplete comments on problems observed are welcomed by planners, who must deal with similar challenges from older citizens. When students have been invited to help with planning activities, when they have proved themselves useful and are not too unpleasantly opinionated, they are welcomed by planners.

Improving Race Relations

Here indeed is a place where college-age youth can do great harm if they uncritically follow their generous impulses. It is clear that the vast majority of American communities have much to learn about decency of treatment for minorities. It is equally clear that older residents resent pressure for rapid reform in this field from those they regard as inexperienced, those who are "foolishly unaware of the facts of life."

In such a controversial field we have concluded that action in the community undertaken by students alone almost always leads to unfortunate results. When, however, students can meet with committees of well-established residents, they can help to work out realistic steps for the alleviation of prejudice. Such activities as the promotion of interracial and interreligious meetings and projects and the improvement of housing for disadvantaged minorities are within the realm of possibility. These will not bring in utopia overnight. But they will allow that progress which will be tolerated by a community, while teaching young people to take responsibility for an important phase of citizenship.

Attendance at Meetings

Although students "earn" their right to take part in policymaking by hard work, their best learning of citizenship comes in attendance at discussion meetings with responsible adults. There is nothing quite so characteristic of American democracy as the discussion meeting. The citizen who complains that he is weary of endless and perpetual meetings is expressing a critical comment universal in all functioning democracies. The young should be initiated early in a wearisome but necessary activity. If meetings are slow or seemingly arrive at no conclusions, students should learn that such things are part of a way of life to which they give thoughtless assent. They may also, out of such experience, study means for increasing the efficiency and productivity of the meeting as a device for group thinking.

The privilege of attending meetings comes by invitation from the community. No educational institution should assume that its students will be welcome merely because it has young people to educate in citizenship. Students are welcomed in meetings because they have proved themselves useful. We have found that we must sometimes wait for years before a particular community will overcome its suspicion of "callow" students and "impractical" professors. Learners were finally welcome only after successful work in other communities and after discovery of some local task at which they could labor usefully.

The attendance at formal meetings of a city council, state legislature, or court of law is good but insufficient for adequate learning. Familiarity with such legally proper functions is necessary, but limited for the understanding of democratic process. More important is the intimate discussion that may occur in small planning commission or committee of a larger body or in the nonofficial amateur organization. The church group, women's club, service club, labor union, or the combination of these in a community council will illustrate better the processes of personal interreaction which are essential to successful democracy. Education for democratic citizenship must extend far beyond the workings of formal, legal government.

DISCUSSION-CENTERED DEMOCRACY

It has long been traditional to point to the ballot box in a free election as the characteristic symbol of free democracy. The more accurate functioning symbol for our time is the meeting, endlessly attended in most communities. Unfortunately, the word "meeting" is used to describe a large variety of occasions when people congregate in the same room. We prefer to limit use to the situation in which several people come together to solve some problem, exchange differing opinions, and if possible arrive at some course of action. It is not primarily a social event. There should be a minimum of speechmaking. Ideally, everyone present both speaks and listens; the group does not divide itself into speakers and audience. Frequently the "called" formal meetings of some organization will illustrate the ideal less than the casual coming together of friends or of a small committee.

Often participants in small gatherings will be less impressed with the informal but serious meeting than with some big, well-advertised, and well-attended event. Yet here is the place at which antagonistic factions or persons may meet to iron out their differences. Here is the place in which group thinking can occur. Here fundamental policy is often hammered out, for later formal adoption in huge convention or election. The often-derided meeting for serious business is or can become the creative center of the process by which free society matures. The discussion process which takes place at such an occasion is important. It needs to be studied and made more efficient. Future citizens should be trained as skillful participants in discussion, which is the essence of the successful meeting.

The smoke-filled hotel rooms in which real decisions are made have long been condemned by moralists who view political conventions with alarm. Perhaps the cause of democratic maturity would be better served if such small meetings were accepted as a necessary part of the machinery of policymaking and tamed to serve the public interest. It is seldom that a huge assemblage like the convention of a political party can think through problems to reach a conclusion. Such a mass conglomeration can only endorse or reject decisions already reached by smaller groups. The real exchange and integration of opinion occur in face-to-face exchanges, whether the air be polluted by the smoke of selfish interest or purified by the breeze of highest idealism. Even the much-challenged "horse-trading" deal by which rival interests come to terms may at times illustrate the fine art of compromise as a result of discussion. All that is needed is to open the discussion to a wider range of interests, more representative of the public good, and to insist that reports back to larger assemblages be as honest as possible. The citizen of the future needs to possess both understanding of and skill in the processes by which decisions are formulated and later endorsed.

Skill as a discussant comes in part from attendance at community meetings. Exchange of opinion in analysis which gives meaning to community experience adds more. The virtue of work for the common good is educationally limited unless subjected to discussional digestion.

Discussion becomes the process by which education for future citizenship is guided. Through it, students are led to assume responsibility both for community projects and for their own curriculum of learning. In the absence of a textbook or syllabus of citizenship, this is most important. Students, like adults in the community, become to some extent directors of their own growth.

Analysis of Experience

Before each practical experience in a real-life laboratory, it is possible to examine the situation into which the learner is about to be plunged. This investigation includes a collection of all available facts about social forces and factions as well as personalities to be met. It includes an attempt to anticipate how each person will behave, as well as a prediction of several possible outcomes for the meeting. Above all, it includes an analysis of how the situation will be shifted by the arrival of the young learners themselves and a decision as to what "our" attitude and contribution should be. All this analysis is accomplished in the midst of a good-humored exchange of opinion. In this, there is opportunity for dispassionate examination of other people and of one's own self. This is the pre-analysis.

After attendance at the meeting, the post-analysis takes place. Frequently it will be found that the pre-analysis was faulty and that unpredicted developments took place. The question then arises, "Wherein did our anticipatory understanding fail? Can we learn from this in order to be more adequate next time?"

There is obvious room for difference of opinion in such a process of experience-plus-discussion. The difference is all the more obvious since there is no correct or final answer for the many questions which inevitably are raised. No professor can pose as expert-with-all-the-answers. Conclusions can therefore be reached by consensus, a most important feature of discussion.

Meaningful Use of References

Soon even those students who ordinarily resist learning find that they do not know enough to have intelligent opinions or to join in a defensible consensus. This realization makes the use of reference material seem most obvious. There is then a willingness to study pertinent books and pamphlets. Knowledge has a relevance to a problem to be solved. Frequently, too, communities in need of data for decisions will turn to students for help. The latter then see that information must be assembled in response to expressed need. Students, with the help of the college instructors, have already been called upon to organize information for community committees on such diverse matters as:

An outline of youth development and needs for a program of parent education.

Listings of help in the field of recreation.

Historical maps of a town's development.

Land-use data, collected and coded according to the best practice of experienced city planners.

Preparation of questionnaires and interview schedules for surveys.

Advice on how to handle a program of public relations.

Information on sewage disposal.

Experience of businesses with the employment and upgrading of disadvantaged minorities.

Help in organizing and conducting community councils.

The fact that obviously inexperienced students are requested to provide help to mature adults on such questions is evidence of the vitality of matters discussed. In collecting data for answers students find a practical utility for research.

Promotional Activities

Discussion has another utility than the mere meeting of minds. It can be used also to stir them up. This is the promotional function. Students learning to become democratic leaders will not be content to wait for requests for help to come to them. Or when decisions are lost in apathy, or moving in the "wrong" direction, they cannot be expected to sit idly by. Do they then become promoters and manipulators? Discussion is the process by which the "high-pressure selling" phases of promotion can be avoided. There can be a pushing for different points of view or better action, but action occurs only after others are convinced and make the changed proposition their own. Persuasion that avoids propaganda and coercion is necessary for mature democracy.

Perhaps the most tragic community of all is that one in which there is no common meeting ground for discussion to take place. Again and again we have found American towns in which there is a hopeless determination to do nothing because of indifference, previous failure, or inability to cooperate. The democratic process is at low ebb. There is need for someone to promote, not a specific program of improvement, but a method by which a program can be thought through and acted upon. This is an approach most difficult to learn in the age of advertising to "sell" specific panaceas. The democratic citizen of the future needs to be a promoter, that is, a salesman of democratic processes. How people may be brought together and stimulated to discuss their problems and hopes is one of the basic obligations of education for citizenship.

Students in training for future citizenship learn to become promoters of democratic process partly as a result of finding that process vital in their own experience. A class traditionally organized in terms of coercive assignments and motivation provided by threat of examination and failure will not serve this purpose. Such an organization of learning is more consistent with dictatorship. Discussion, with free participation, must be the heart of student experience. Tasks are accepted after consideration pro and con, and assignments are undertaken voluntarily. The coercion is self-coercion. The discipline is the discipline of a responsible group.

PERSONALITIES FOR DEMOCRACY

Undoubtedly certain information is essential for well-trained citizens. But overwhelmingly important are the personality skills required for successful participation in democracy. Knowledge, plus certain attitudes, plus ability to handle characteristic social situations—these are all essential to personalities for democracy.

It is probable that all people connected with educational efforts seek to produce personalities patterned after their own images. Possibly the writer exhibits no exception to this weakness. Since democracy is a developing way of life, it is not easy to predict the kind of personality which will fit best in the future. Perhaps no single type is suitable, not even that modeled after the writer. A variety will make for more vigor in democracy as well as for more interest. Nonetheless, there are certain skills intimately related to personality which, on the basis of our experience, seem worthy of cultivation.

Contrary to the theme of many a self-congratulatory political speech, the vigorous citizen of democracy is constantly pushing for improvement. He is never satisfied with achievements, no matter how remarkable. The orators of complacency, in seeking to build loyalty to American democracy as against all other political philosophies, frequently point with pride to present blessings. These range all the way from a superiority in numbers of telephones and bathtubs to laws and traditions pointing toward great freedom. This is the wrong mood for citizens energetic enough to make democracy survive in trying times. Without meaning to criticize the achievement of the past, the good citizen of the present must work for a better future.

Disciplined Idealism

Fortunately the years of late adolescence and early adulthood are usually characterized by considerable aspiration for social betterment. This tendency can be harnessed for citizenship education.

The fact that the idealistic aspirations of youth are so often stifled is probably traceable to insistence upon purely factual learning plus moral teaching relatively unrelated to the realities of ordinary life. A good educational procedure will seek to utilize youthful hopes and to discipline this motivation by experience with life as it is, in process of becoming something better.

It is probable that many a reformer has done a disservice to the cause he has sought to promote by insisting upon some "perfect" solution to the ills of the human race. Viewing with disapproving eye the obvious injustices of his time, he has created his utopia in imagination, then has insisted that all men must conform to that fixed pattern or be condemned as reactionaries. Religious zealots and political revolutionaries have in common this insistence upon some absolutely "correct" position. They present to eager young people a choice between existing conditions, which they paint as unideal, and a never-never land of perfection, which could not be created even under a dictatorship of the reformers.

The democratic citizen of the future must come to realize that problems are never solved with perfect finality. The ills of men are alleviated, seldom eliminated. Any workable solution to a problem is always a compromise among factional interests, between that which is and that which ought to be. Democracy never arrives; it is always in process. As long as men have freedom there must be room for something less than perfection. Compromise of ideals is not necessarily to be condemned. It may represent the flexibility upon which the progress of free men is based.

The advocates of dictatorship point with pride to the perfection of their slavish utopia and sneer at the way in which a free society inevitably falls short of its ideals. Supporters of democracy should never compete with them to boast of the perfection of achievement; they should rather take pride in perfection of process. Free men can remain free only as they make progress through a series of compromises which satisfy no one completely. To realize and work with this necessity requires self-discipline.

The discipline of idealistic aspiration is not developed by required courses or by imposed assignments. Such teacher-chosen pressures can contribute rather to the development of apathy and cynicism. Discipline grows, instead, out of discoveries stemming from real experience with ideals in action. Among these is likely to be the conclusion that goodness needs the guidance of thought.

It is not enough to be right merely. One needs also to be intelligent. The achievement of any end, however noble, requires careful study and planning. People will not accept an idea merely because it seems obviously correct to those who propose it. Progress comes as a result of joint effort from the heart and the head.

Disciplined Intelligence

A related discipline is that of objectivity. Intelligence operates in social affairs as it is cleared of emotional prejudgments. In order to engage intelligently in projects of community improvement, students must learn to analyze the interests, the factions, and the personalities involved—including themselves. They can learn to assess each for its worth, contribution, and weaknesses. In the discussion, opinions can be offered with no restraint other than reasonable consideration for the feelings of other people. Each student after attendance at the community meeting is asked to write a report on his impressions of events. This sets the stage for coolheaded analysis. When the report is read to the rest of the class, it becomes a basis for discussion. Difference of opinion is encouraged. Ultimate agreement in analysis may be reached but is not imperative. Free men can agree to disagree without rancor. Because expression of opinion is held confidential, it is possible to cultivate objectivity in dealing with real people and real events.

One of the disciplines most difficult to acquire is that of discretion—to learn when to speak, when to remain silent. Many a youth (and adult) is notoriously lacking in this skill. When dealing with real people facing actual situations, however, it becomes apparent almost immediately that an unwise word or action might jeopardize months of careful work. Under these circumstances young people learn discretion fast, because they too are eager to see progress made. Discretion should be based upon social sensitivity, an ability to size up people and their reactions. A sympathetic understanding of the frustrations, the hopes and fears of other people tends to grow out of continued analysis of real observed situations. It is possible to develop an ability to make an increasingly accurate guess about underlying motives. All of us, present adults included, need constant growth in this skill if we are to function successfully in the many meetings which are the heart of democracy. That sensitivity begins to grow in young people as they learn to analyze the meetings they have attended or plan to attend, and to determine the part they shall play.

The Skill of Humor

The great solvent of tension in difficult social situations is humor. Great leaders of democracy have again and again used the well-timed joke. But an active sense of humor involves much more. Beyond the ability to laugh or make others laugh lies the kindly understanding of human frailty and faith in the probability that people's better selves will ultimately triumph over the poorer impulses. Humor therefore develops not out of familiarity with a joke book but out of sympathy not unrelated to objectivity. The wise use of humor calls for skill which citizens of an ongoing democracy need, lest they take themselves and their opponents too seriously. A sense of humor can be cultivated as a result of the confidence which students develop in democratic processes.

Perhaps humor is related to patience. Patience need not be mere stubborn long-suffering. This could easily become an oxlike complacency. The willingness to wait for desired results should grow out of an understanding of the processes which are at work and which will move toward hoped-for ends in time. Students catch the beginnings of learning here by discovery that community processes are slow-moving, that they grow through periods of both intense activity and quiescence. They learn patience further by discovering that challengingly idealistic ends are often reached by going through long days, weeks and months of boring drudgery. The noble ideal and the "leg work" are closely related. A paradox of attitude is called for, a willingness to work hard and continuously coupled with a willingness to wait with undiscouraged patience for long-postponed results.

The results, when they finally emerge, are seldom exactly those which were originally sought by the promoters of improvement. To accept that which is presently possible without the gloom of disappointment, yet to press on for better achievements—this puts any sense of humor to a major test. When balanced perspective takes the place of disappointment, it is sometimes possible to realize that the actual action taken is more satisfactory than any preconceived blueprint. Part of the promise of mature democracy lies in the hope that methods can be worked out whereby the wisdom of many people can be integrated to provide answers to problems better than any one single individual can find.

The neglected aspect of citizenship education for youth lies in the development of personality habits and attitudes. No amount of knowledge of governmental form and legal functioning, necessary though these be, will compensate for lack of skill in dealing with one's fellow human beings. The cultivation of this skill in meetings called to solve problems points toward the democracy of the future.

COMPETITION PLUS INTEGRATION

Whenever men are frightened by crisis, there is an inevitable tendency to look for a strong man to lead them out of the wilderness of uncertainty. They gaze with longing at the Washingtons, Jeffersons, and Lincolns of the past, hoping that another such giant may arise, forgetting that these leaders were not so great in the eyes of their contemporaries. They lose confidence in themselves, or more serious, they lose confidence in their fellow citizens to find the collective wisdom to solve the difficulties of the time.

Such confidence does not grow primarily from preaching about democracy. It comes from the experience of meeting and working with others to grow together in solving all kinds of problems. The oncoming citizen learns this also from actual experience plus study and discussion. He must get such learnings into his muscles and emotions as well as into his head. He learns to have confidence in himself and in others by working with them toward some mutually desired goal.

Americans have found so much satisfaction in a first step in the democratic process that they have failed to press on to the next. They point with legitimate pride to the competition of ideas that comes with freedom of speech, to the vigor of open debate in newspaper or legislative hall. But free nations are vulnerable to criticism because they have failed to move on to the next essential stage. Critics point out that energetic competition of opinion delays and confuses decisions that are taken quickly by totalitarian powers. And then, when at last a policy is adopted, there is usually a disgruntled minority which was outvoted and which gives only half-hearted support. The unrealized next step, which promises to strengthen democracies against such criticism, is the learning of a technique of integration of freely expressed oppositions. Without diminishing the vigor of free debate, it is possible to find a consensus which will benefit by the contributed wisdom of all thoughtful debaters. Skill in such integration is learned first in the face-to-face relationships of meetings working on problems of local improvement.

It is not enough to train the young with the less mature citizens of today as models. Let them be trained in anticipation of the next necessary steps toward maturation of democracy.

In the final analysis, it is not possible to teach democratic citizenship. It is possible only to expose the oncoming generation to it. Personalities for maturing democracy grow through carefully chosen experiences that help produce self-discipline. You cannot force freedom. You can only invite it.

CHAPTER VI

Training Community Educators

WHEN a student goes on to graduate school after completing a liberal arts education, he may suspect uneasily that his next experiences will be repetitious. When we offer graduate studies looking toward a master's degree in community dynamics are we providing only a continuation of Earlham undergraduate education for future citizens—more of the same but a bit more intense? In part, yes. But there is something beyond this in the process and in the outcome sought. Undergraduate training is directed toward future citizens whatever their vocations. The graduate training is for professionals who expect to make their living as community educators.

The problem of a name for such professionals is a serious one. The difficulty goes beyond the inadequacy of words. It is related to a widespread American fear of having one's own personality invaded by those who would "educate," cajole, or "sell" one on otherwise unacceptable ideas. The terms "teacher" or "education" are good, but to many they carry an unpleasant aroma. The suspicion prevails that when a person becomes a community educator he or she hopes to tell others how to organize their lives. The term "community organizer" has even more doubtful meanings. In many minds it has become associated with charitable welfare work, a caring for the unfortunate, not a better self-development by responsible normal people. In other minds it is related to "high-pressure" methods often used in financial campaigns.

Despite unfortunate connotations we would like to rescue and use the term "community educator." In doing so, we refer to the original Latin meaning; to educate is to "lead out." The terms "catalyst," "guide," or "consultant" could be regarded as synonyms. We hope that we are training teaching leaders of a growing, dynamic democracy.

TEACHING LEADERS

The word "leader" is here being used in a somewhat specialized sense. Reference is not made to the great personality usually found in democracy's yesterday, or to the salesman of specific panaceas characteristic of democracy's today, or to the humble leader who emerges from community growth for democracy's tomorrow. We refer now to a promoter of individual and social growth, who seeks to produce humble leaders, a few of whom might in time become great personalities.

A comment upon the salesman for specific panaceas would be appropriate. The self-advertising seeker for power or propagandist for economic or political faiths is obvious enough for general condemnation. But his unpleasant methods of salesmanship are more readily tolerated when they are used to gain support for some genuinely worthy cause. The nation is filled with community organizers trying to "sell the public" on support for some specific noble purpose. There are organizers for support of social work agencies, for health programs, for adult education, for better race relations, and many more. In the health field alone, not only are there rival organizers for health prepayment plans and for disaster relief, but national committees are set up in the name of particular diseases to gain public support for each. There is a tuberculosis organization, a polio organization, a cancer organization, and so on, all competing with one another and with promoters of adult education, recreation, and religious organizations for public interest and contribution. All these are to be commended for their ultimate objectives. Are they to be approved for their methods of promotion?

Although a community educator might find himself employed as a promoter-salesman-organizer for some specific interest, it is our purpose to train broader-scale "generalists." Our professionally trained people should be able to adapt themselves to highly specific efforts, but they have a more fundamental and more difficult job to learn. We make it a point to avoid their becoming professionals in health, recreation, et al. They should become skilled in dealing with the complications of human relations. In order to be successful in this intricate field, they must avoid the appearance of professional skill. They must seem and must actually be friendly people, meeting others on a kindly level of human sharing. In being "generalists" they avoid the professional manner, which becomes deplorable when either perfunctory or over-profound.

Ordinary citizens need to cultivate a deeper understanding of the emotions and inner thoughts of other people. Yes, but the teaching leader should be a top-ranking expert in this matter. The purpose is not to play upon human motivation and weakness in "putting over" a campaign but to help people grow in self-motivated maturity. When adroit psychological tricks are used to gain adherence to any project, the people thus played upon are weakened, even though the project be good. When people think through their needs and consciously adopt a project, then evaluate their success in carrying it to completion, they become stronger. More skill is needed to help people grow in responsibility than is required to manipulate them for ends they have not themselves chosen.

Throughout history there have arisen occasional geniuses who were untaught psychologists able to manipulate their fellows for their own ends. Usually their purposes have been the selfish ends of personal power. The twentieth century has seen the development of a systematic psychology turned to the training of those with commercial intent. The proponents of good will have borrowed from these highly successful manipulators. In the training of community educators we merely insist that as much understanding of human behavior be utilized, to help people become stronger in self-chosen responsibility.

Growth toward such maturity may often go through phases when the learner is scarcely conscious of his own need and progress. Ultimately, if successful, the learner becomes aware of and helps guide the process.

The white chairman of an interracial community council described to two graduate students how he had come to accept Negroes as fellow human beings following upon certain joint activities. "Say," he said suddenly, "have you guys been working on me to change my point of view on this?"

"Yes," said one of the students.

"Well, guess that's all right"—with a grin. "I've been watching how you guys operate, and we're all better off anyway."

The end sought is the development of stronger citizens, who are conscious of the process of growth by which they mature, who participate more and more in the process. Psychological skill to promote such learning is not easy to teach. But it can be done.

A Professional Curriculum

How can such skill be taught? Not by courses in psychological or sociological principles. Rather by experience in dealing with people in such a fashion that the principles become operative. During two years of graduate study the student accepts responsibility for guiding the learning process, for undergraduates, for emerging community leaders. He does whatever is necessary to expedite the projects under way. He may help in the organization of committees, in conducting a survey, in working on a cleanup, in repairing homes. He gains skill in guidance of people by working with people. He works himself but he encourages others to work also.

Out of experience gained by guiding learning projects actually in progress, this student discovers that he must be familiar with certain technical skills. These may include historical research, map making, discussion leadership, creation of questionnaires, the technique of surveys, statistical manipulations, and others. Useful as these are, they are tools only. One should be able to use them when necessary, not become a slave to them. The impedimenta of research and scientific method, painfully conceived, can become a barrier between ordinary people and the would-be community educator. Better to hold these skills in the background until they can expedite some vital activity. Better to teach them in relationship to ongoing projects, not as separate elements of a curriculum to be admired in their own right.

Instead of conceiving of scientific method as a straitjacket of techniques to be strapped on to every community, it is better to consider how the scientific spirit can be adapted to the doings of ordinary folk. This involves the promotion of an experimental view of life. Leaders must be prepared to try out several different possible solutions, being unfrightened by the fact that the first or second attempt results in something less than success. The community educator should be prepared to encourage this willingness to try a wide variety of possible solutions to problems.

Action-Research Methodology

A particular adaptation of the scientific spirit to the affairs of ordinary people needs to be learned. This is action-research methodology, applied to communities.

Traditionally, investigators of community life have been content to investigate and carefully describe a situation, in the typical community survey. It results in description impressive to the social scientist, or one which could be used as basis for a program of improvement, or one which might be filed away to gather dust until no longer significant. It represents a single compilation of facts, accurate perhaps and free from prejudice, but limited to a particular time or stage of development.

The action-research method is dynamic. It covers a period of time, showing growth. It is a technique not for describing things as they are but for examining the process by which they arrived at that point and continue to change.

When a community is chosen as social unit for study, a beginning is selected at some stage of development in time. Historical material is collected and some description of present conditions obtained. This provides a starting point. It is important, however, that no outside scientific body or person decide to conduct a survey prior to a decision to collect such information on the part of a community committee. In one community we made the unhappy mistake of collecting data in a survey on our own initiative. We later had much to explain and anxious moments while we sought to reestablish our acceptability as co-learners. If the scientific spirit is to spread, ordinary people must become participants in the research. The catalyst-leader as researcher picks up and records information from day-by-day contacts, gradually involving citizens in this as rapidly as they find such activity rewarding. A tentative description of the community is needed as starting point. This should be amplified and modified continually and cooperatively as time goes on.

The catalyst promotes change, the organization of a council, the decision to attempt work on some project. He recognizes that his arrival on the scene itself constitutes one change. He observes and records the success or failure flowing from the change; he looks especially for results of any action taken. Over a period of time he comes up with a flowing, dynamic description of a community in action, in process of change. Historical descriptions, surveys, opinions about the community may all be part of the record. But they are now placed in a sequence of events in process of growth. It is possible to observe progress or the lack of progress, over a period of time.

The catalyst-leader, in promoting the scientific spirit, may also help develop an important contribution to scientific research. This is the self-observation, by local citizens, of the growth of themselves and their community. Skill to promote this is best taught to future community educators by their taking part in actual action-research.

Personality Skills for the Community Educator

All the personality skills possessed by citizens should be accentuated in the catalyst-teacher, for he is an inspirer of citizens. But he should acquire some additional abilities.

Among the first he should learn to make himself personally acceptable. There are those who seem to know how to put themselves and others at ease, even in strange company, without planning out a campaign of approach. Although a friendly manner may be God-given in some people, it can be learned. Moreover, those who have learned it the hard way are probably more flexible in adapting their manner, in varying the approach according to the group. The extroverted manner which is acceptable in the luncheon-service club of businessmen is ill-adapted to a ladies' missionary society.

Then the community educator should persuade people to have confidence in him. Again, although there are those with God-given characteristics here, the ability to create confidence can be cultivated. A calm, unworried manner of meeting the most serious problems, an assurance that one has contended with situations like this before, a sense of humor which may quietly relieve tense moments—these are all tricks of the trade which can be learned. They are learned best by observation and exercise in action.

"How did you know what to do?" asked a graduate student of a staff member in post-analysis of a community meeting.

"I did not know what to do," was the reply.

"Well, you acted like you did."

"You mean I tried to act as though I was sure that some solution to the problem would be worked out. I tried to create a feeling of confidence which would encourage the people to have confidence in themselves."

Placing confidence in a catalyst-teacher is often preliminary to building confidence in oneself and one's group.

Another closely related skill is the ability to listen, carefully and intelligently. This is more than the closed mouth, the open ear, and the attentive manner. Listening to good purpose involves learning about the other fellow's worries and hopes, forming surmises as to his frustrations and motivations, picking up clues as to positive actions to be proposed. Intelligent listening, punctuated by brief remarks that indicate understanding, is the beginning of a creative process. Judicious questioning to encourage emergence of more material for listening is a next step. "Bringing a person out" is the end result sought, especially important for those who do not speak easily, or for those who lack confidence in their own ideas.

Perhaps all these suggestions seem to fall under the head of tact or diplomacy. If so, many assume that social skill is inborn. The evidence does not support such a fatalistic position. Tact in dealing with people can be cultivated in the process of dealing with people.

For some, diplomacy has a mildly unpleasant sound. It suggests "pulling the wool over people's eyes" in order to "put something over on them." It is a wry commentary upon our civilization that so often it is assumed that a person who is attentive and pleasant has some ulterior and selfish motive. When we have been called into a community and have offered to be helpful, we have often been greeted by the questions:

"What's the catch?"

"What do we have to do for you?"

In all fairness it must be admitted that those who will be nice for an expected consideration are more numerous than those who adopt the same manner in order to help the other fellow mature. Whatever the limitations of our civilization or of people's expectations, the community catalyst should be trained to be diplomatic in being helpful.

The Technique of Self-Effacement

Any good teacher finds his major satisfaction in the growth of the taught. The community catalyst is no exception. The term "catalyst" needs a special definition in human relations. The dictionary defines a catalytic agent as a substance which by its presence accelerates a reaction or process while itself remaining unchanged. It is too much to expect that any human being dealing with other human beings will remain unchanged in the process. He may put up the appearance of imperturbability. Indeed, this is recommended as he takes the role of accelerator or precipitator of action and growth in others. But he is a catalyst who changes with the process.

So easy is it to bask in the glow of compliments for a few things accomplished in a community that a definite technique of self-effacement needs to be taught. This is particularly necessary since the process of local growth must often start with the teacher-catalyst assuming a much too prominent role. There are frequently definite stages of human catalytic action.

1. At the beginning of work in a community the guide may be more the "telling" teacher and less the stimulating expediter. People are lacking in confidence and bereft of ideas. They tend to lean upon someone who seems to be strong. They are frequently astounded at their own accomplishments and tend to give credit to the inspirer of the work despite his refusal to accept credit. He may, in order to encourage others, point out his own weaknesses and failures in a humorous way. This is not self-effacement yet. It is a process of drawing attention to oneself in a derogatory way in order to encourage others to try themselves out, despite lack of confidence.

2. Gradually, confidence increases with accomplishment. Community members are willing to take a little more and a little more responsibility. The teacher becomes more the catalyst, taking less initiative, raising questions and offering suggestions mainly. He sees that credit is given to people who have shown initiative, perhaps even beyond their deserving.

3. Finally, community members are ready to take over the planning and responsibility for projects themselves. They should receive full credit for all work done. The catalyst becomes an adviser only, expecting to have his suggestions voted down a good part of the time, expecting to have them adopted only on their merit, not on his prestige.

The steps outlined represent merely the beginning phases. The catalyst remains in contact with community progress indefinitely after he has reduced himself to proper size. He remains a suggester and stimulator, from the background, and idea man who nonetheless can be put in his place if need be.

The Art of Timing

The difficult and important art of timing cannot be taught, partly because no one is wise enough to know just when important but potentially fatal moves should be made. So uncertain are these matters and so dependent upon fallible human judgment that decisions should be made prayerfully and with the fingers crossed. But if the uncertainty is too obvious, that fact alone may foredoom the move to failure. It becomes necessary, therefore, to adopt a manner of calm confidence, whatever the inward vacillation.

Again we have historical and contemporary records of men who seem to have had a remarkable "natural" ability to time their public statements and moves. Politicians who remain successful over a period of time seem either to have or to develop skills in this field, probably as an outgrowth of the much-to-be-admired sensitivity to other people's development, needs, moods. Although certain leaders may start with an initial handicap over their fellows, we are convinced that social sensitivity can be cultivated. We see no way to do this adequately except by taking part in social growth, by analyzing the process through discussion with those involved, by learning from both mistakes and successes.

Any attempt to supervise a learning process of either students or citizens forces the matter of timing to the attention of the community educator-in-training. We have discovered that an idea proposed at one time in a community will fall on deaf ears, whereas the same idea proposed later will be taken up with enthusiasm. Often it will be reproposed by those who rejected it earlier. It is moreover unwise to push for certain projects when the situation is not ripe for such activities. Psychologists tell us that individual learning takes place when there is a readiness on the part of the learner. There must be a readiness in committees, councils, and communities too, without which no learning, or the wrong learning, will take place. Community catalysts must learn to recognize and utilize the tide in the affairs of men that leads on to maturity.

THE COMMUNITY EDUCATOR AT WORK

To eyes clouded by some of the ungenerous impulses of a society of salesmanship, it still may seem that we are merely training adroit manipulators. We believe that we are trying to develop in the promoters of maturity a skill as great as is to be found in less generously motivated manipulators of men. Success is measured in terms of men's freedom to act according to their own decisions.

Sometimes students new to community learning processes make the horrible accusation of manipulation. This arises in their thinking when citizens make the decision we had hoped they might make, or when some committee adopts as its own an idea which we had proposed months before. The community educator should freely and openly admit his intention to influence others. The real question is whether the persons influenced are made more independent in the process. No one is completely original in ideas. We all borrow from someone. The citizen may get ideas in a meeting, from his reading, from casual conversation, or from a radio program. The crux of the matter is, Does he adopt them as his own in a rational fashion, before he acts? If he does, then the fact that he received the original inspiration from us rather than from someone else is not important. The test of democratic process is the human product.

If the work of the community educator be manipulation, it is the kind that notifies its "victims" of the process. It encourages citizens to build defenses against becoming pawns, even in the hands of people like himself. It seeks to make them cooperators in self-manipulation.

Perhaps the point and the picture can be made sharper by asking how a community catalyst actually works. The preliminary steps have been suggested. If he comes anew into a community, he may have to spend weeks or months in friendly efforts to gain acceptance as a human being to be trusted. He then finds or helps form some council, committee, or combination of several groups which can be encouraged to grow in responsibility as it plans for the general welfare.

Diplomacy in Action

After the phase has been passed when the catalyst must be over-prominent, the important and difficult and more permanent educational job begins. What are his responsibilities? The first job is to sit intelligently quiet in a meeting. This is not easy. To be attentive, to analyze inwardly the events, personalities, and tensions observed, and to hold one's peace until the time has arrived for action requires much self-discipline. Then to decide whether the situation calls for an offhand humorous remark, the mention of a challenging question, or a full-scale outburst of eloquence requires skilled judgment. The successful catalyst must learn to hold his enthusiasm in abeyance when it is inappropriate and yet have it on tap ready to effervesce, not when he is in the mood, but when those in the meeting are ready to respond.

The catalyst acts as a guide mainly by raising questions and making suggestions in a tentative tone of voice. If these are not picked up and developed by others, he drops them and waits without resentment. If the suggestions are pertinent to meet real needs, they may reappear later in the proposals of organization members with no credit offered to the catalyst. The good educator rejoices, even though his suggestion may have been considerably modified in process of digestion. He seeks no credit for himself. Rather he is gratified to find his suggestions reincarnated in the thinking of others. The end he is seeking is that proposals shall be acted upon because they are genuinely a part of the thinking of citizens, whatever the original source of inspiration. The growth sought is the ability to seek new ideas, examine these critically, and adopt them in an experimental mood.

Sometimes the catalyst attempts to warn away from ill-considered action. Though the warning may go unheeded, it should be made. One community council, on breathless demand of a veterans' group, insisted upon beginning the erection of a community building before legal title to the land had been cleared. Our warnings went unheeded. The half-completed building, as a consequence, stood for months, a monument of futility. But the warning of impending failure kept the council from disintegrating.

The guidance function calls for many delicate and difficult decisions. Here is a community council possessing a chairman who is an extroverted enthusiast. To put it bluntly, he talks too much. Discussion tends to be stifled by his ready, and usually pertinent, comment upon every issue that comes up. Yet the council needs the energy of his pushing personality. Should the catalyst attempt to instruct him in the arts of discussion, or would this apparent criticism dampen his enthusiasm too much? Or would it be better to allow negative comments from the group to have effect upon him? There is always danger that an excess of negative reaction may lead to a breakup of the council. A gently persuasive approach, salted with kindly humor, frequently will be able to diminish the chairman's readiness to speak and increase the tendency of others to have their say. This possibly can be handled by quiet personal conversation. But there is no sure-fire formula that guarantees results.

Warnings

The community educator is human. He is subject to temptations and prone to error like all mortal flesh. Certain dangers can be pointed out to learners and to experienced old hands.

Avoid the painfully superior attitude of the person with noble motives. There is a subtle form of domination in the approach of one who is determined to improve people with or without their consent. There is an implication of superiority either through knowledge and skill or, much worse, through good intention. It is seldom possible to work *on* self-respecting people. With understanding skill it is often possible to work *with* people, to grow with them. The catalyst must become a participant in the activity and learning, but a participant with some inward reserve. The reserve is an inward critical judgment on events and people, an ability to analyze objectively. This is a skill possessed by all thoughtful people in at least rudimentary form.

The Biblical advice, "Judge not that ye be not judged," is important here. People are to be treated as human beings with infinite possibilities, whatever their present weaknesses or past misdemeanors. Are all organizations equally acceptable in a community council? We have taken the position that the community educator must work with all factions and organizations whether or not he agrees with their policies and practices. There is, of course, an extreme limit for such cooperation which must be determined by the ethical standards of both community and guide. We, for example, advised a council (at their request) to refuse contributions from the organized liquor interests of a town. We did this not because we feared "tainted" money but because the liquor-plus-vice interests sought public approval by giving to a good cause.

We would not refuse contacts with individuals, even those of doubtful reputation. After all, they too are human beings with the ability to grow. We would avoid the seeming endorsement of organizations which are illegal or clearly antisocial. The dividing line between the acceptable and the nonacceptable in organizations is exceedingly hard to designate. Up to that line, wherever it is drawn, we would "judge not" but would advise inclusion of all in a community council. Our own distaste or doubts we would hold in abeyance while we worked with people to discover better motives in them.

Often the guide will find that his conclusions are at variance with those of emerging community leaders, particularly when attempting to decide upon some problem which is to become the basis for a project. The community educator may discover certain, to him, obvious needs which cry out for corrective activity. The council and its leaders may prove uninterested and fasten their attention upon some comparatively insignificant issue. The necessities of growth call for the educator again to hold his views in abeyance, hoping that the council will eventually grow in appreciation of the greater problems he can see. The most he should do to expedite the process is raise questions and make quiet, casual suggestions. He looks for evidence of awakening conscience and expanding insight but must never force an acceptance of his project, whatever the obvious merits thereof. The community educator is merely an adjunct who can speed or retard a process, depending upon skill.

Anyone who attempts to fill the role of catalyst successfully must become a part of a social process, yet remain inwardly apart from it. Especially must he hold himself in check when newly developed leaders have acquired sufficient self-confidence to ask for no more help. Then to remain in the picture at all may require diplomacy. To stand by and see inexperienced people make unwise decisions requires major patience and faith in people's ability to learn from failure.

Above all, the guide needs a genuine humbleness to learn. His experience may be extensive, but frequently he will find that community activities develop in unpredictable, but desirable, ways. There is as yet no correct course for community development to follow. The wisest of us can learn from the unique characteristics of each new situation.

There is no formula for handling delicate human situations in the interest of maximum growth for all. There is no training for this field but actual experience plus discussional analysis based upon study of pertinent scientific thinking. The community educator deals with one of the most delicate and complicated of processes, human social growth. He must become a top-grade expert in a process which depends finally on the initiative of the learner. This is the *method of encouragement.*

CHAPTER VII

The Method of Encouragement

HOW do you change people? People do change—in behavior, in thinking, in loyalties. Can they be influenced toward the objectives which would-be leaders "know" are good? This is a question of interest to politicians, merchants, ministers, teachers, parents, children—in short, to all of us. Most of us agree that people need changing, especially folks other than ourselves. We will sometimes agree that we ourselves need some reorganization. But the admission is usually abstract and seldom refers to any specific weakness that needs correction.

Our answer to the question is not concerned with physical coercion as a method of changing people. In response to force, people will often do as they are told, without necessarily being reorganized inwardly. Even those experts in coercion, the dictators, found that secret police and concentration camps had to be supplemented with the less obvious methods of propaganda and indoctrination.

The methods of indoctrination do not interest us either. These represent coercion of the mind instead of the body. In addition to stunting the personality stature of those being influenced, indoctrination tends to be ineffective unless addressed to the defenseless young or unless it enjoys a monopoly of persuasion for adults. Schools, churches, newspapers, radios—all need to say the same thing in order to make indoctrination successful with adults. This method has been used effectively by certain religious groups working upon young children. These, as they grow older, often give sincere lip service to the approved creed. But both understanding and the motivation to carry the creed into practice have been lacking.

We are seeking, rather, methods consistent with freedom, with deep-running motivation that leads to action. Freedom is based upon the assumption that more than one choice of belief and action is available. It is further based upon the more courageous assumption that when men are free to select among several alternatives they will ultimately make the best choice. As Lincoln noted, "You cannot fool all the people all the time." But can those who oppose the unworthily ambitious sit back and wait for the ultimate processes of freedom to work? In the much-publicized race between education and catastrophe, catastrophe seems to be winning too much of the time.

Then perhaps the question about changing people can be rephrased: How do you persuade people to want to do that which they ought to do? This is a problem for the sincere believer in growing democracy. It is a problem for all of us. For all of us seek some changes which we are convinced ought to come about.

PERSUASION THAT TAKES ADVANTAGE OF FREEDOM

There are certain methods for influencing other people which are consistent with democracy. Some of these take advantage of freedom but do nothing to improve that freedom. Most of the "high-pressure," organized persuasions of modern times belong in this category.

Argument as a method of influencing people is of ancient lineage and of proved ineffectiveness. It has been abandoned by all the professional persuaders of modern times except lawyers in court or legislators (who are mostly lawyers) when working upon each other. Or it will be used for that small minority in the population who believe they are moved by intelligence, such as professors and writers of books about influencing people.

Argument frequently produces an unhappy result. The persuadee comes to resent the attempt to change him; it is all so obvious. This is the outcome whether the effort is made by one man "buttonholing" another in private conversation, by one faction seeking to win over another in a committee meeting, or by a professional persuader seeking support for a political party through printed material. The successful arguer usually loses the argument, in the resulting resentment.

Mass Persuasion

The profession of public persuasion has sought to reach a deeper level of personality by playing upon widely experienced emotions.

This is the business of the advertiser and propagandist. By some comical quirk of our thinking, the former is held in general good repute, while the latter is frequently condemned. Or his product, propaganda, is looked upon as a dangerous poison to be withheld from a defenseless public. Actually advertising is but one form of propaganda, the kind that notifies the recipient that someone is attempting to change him. And propaganda itself is no more than organized persuasion.

Contemporary organizers of persuasion dub themselves "public relations experts," preferring to avoid the unpleasant term "propagandist." That such a profession should arise was perhaps inevitable in the history of democratic nations, as more and more people obtained the right to vote. That the level of appeal should reach a low common denominator of nearly universal emotion was equally inevitable. The methods which changed men so that they came to purchase quantities of cigarettes or vitamin pills have been applied to support of candidates for political office or to soliciting contributions of money for socially useful purposes.

The freedom of democracy guarantees the right to propagandize. Neither poor taste and bad manners nor the spreading of persuasive appeals in support of causes which you and I condemn should call for censorship. To have the eye and ear offended by the brash and crude is one of the prices modern man must pay for his freedom. The answer lies not in curtailment but in encouragement for more points of view to present themselves. It lies even more in the achievement of higher standards of persuasion which will be forced by development of adults mature enough to think for themselves. The methods of modern propaganda take advantage of freedom; they do little to strengthen people to live in the midst of freedom. Men have been, are being, changed by skillful professional persuaders. Are they becoming pawns of mass manipulators in the process?

Propaganda of the Event

There is more to mass persuasion than production of printed material, or movies, or radio broadcasts. There is the creation and manipulation of events. Certainly the American people during the first half of the twentieth century have responded with radical changes to the propaganda of events. One world war, followed by the worst depression in history, followed by a more alarming second world war, followed by an era of international and domestic tension, has shocked them out of isolationist self-contemplation into unpredictable new ways of thinking and acting.

Those who feel able to anticipate the future can sometimes wait for events to change men according to heart's desire. But most leaders either doubt their prophetic insight or lack confidence in the beneficial effect of the events they foresee. They therefore seek to influence events that these may influence changes in men and women.

It is scarcely news that modern warmakers seek support for their invasions of other nations by creating "incidents." On a smaller scale, domestic would-be persuaders create events in the hope that the resulting news will properly affect public thinking. A picket line in connection with a strike or a protest meeting properly reported— both have such purpose. The properly timed arrival and departure of "big-name" persons can be turned to endorsement of particular propagandas. Community planners use events such as the well-publicized mass meeting or the survey, involving a number of citizens, to stir up interest and gain support.

More important than the propaganda of the event is the interpretation of the event. Even a well-planned future has a disconcerting way of getting out of hand. But the event that turns out "wrong" can often be explained away if one can offer a plausible interpretation. Dictators holding a monopoly of interpretation can explain defeats into victories until the defeats actually come home. No such monopoly exists in a democratic nation. But a newly powerful type of person has appeared upon the scene with the era of the radio: the news commentator. He seems to wield a unique power based upon the admiration of a faithful following which waits for the appointed time each evening to hear the familiar voice. The editorial writer of yesteryear might well envy the influence of the editorializing radio commentator. Many other interpreters there are, most of whom must content themselves with a lesser influence. Anyone seeking to change people by response to events needs to look to the interpretation of events by those who have the already established channels to public attention.

These are currently popular means of changing people. They take advantage of freedom. They are the means for changing men in the mass. Perhaps it was inevitable that in the youth of democracy would-be controllers of their fellows should arise, who were dazzled by the possibility of mass manipulation. Democracy is young; it has before it centuries of growth before it approaches its full potential.

To turn over political decision to ordinary men and women was a new experience. No wonder, perhaps, that an early reaction was the development of devices to change the millions according to the purposes of self-appointed controllers.

The promoter of social improvement, whether in local community or on national and international scale, must use many of the devices of mass persuasion. No matter how noble his motives, he is in competition with many another propagandist for public attention and the development of new affections and habits. He falls short of his noblest motives, however, if he is merely content with the success of his mass persuasive efforts. He should also be pressing constantly for methods of influencing people which increase freedom as well as exploit it.

THE UNIQUENESS OF THE INDIVIDUAL

The socially aware community educator will be continually searching within the mass for the individuals, whose infinite variety tends to be lost in the statistical total. There are difficulties in this search. It is easier to address appeals for change to a least common denominator of emotion than to seek out each separate person. The technical devices of communication provided by modern invention make broadcasting possible to ever larger audiences of passive recipients. The rediscovery and development of individuals strong enough to mature democracy call for invention of social devices and skills to match the technical gadgets.

As long as we deal with huge masses of people in attempting to influence change, the persuasive efforts will tend to reduce men and women to a passive and irresponsible role. The persuadee will develop more and more that characteristic frustration which grows from the feeling of being a pawn in a game played by others, who make the real decisions. The social devices which can rediscover the individual must be found in the smaller group. Hence the importance of perfecting the face-to-face meeting in community, in industry, in situations of conflict, as an instrument for promoting growth of personality.

People can be changed without having their personalities pushed into a diminuendo. They can be persuaded to do that which they ought to do—according to their own better insights. The problem is to improve the insights. The problem is also to discover means for encouraging each person to grow from within, according to his own best motives. Imaginative social experiment is needed to solve these problems.

Human Motive Power

Can the motives of ordinary men be trusted? Are men not selfish, stupid, and subject to the sweeps of mass emotion? Perhaps. But are the motives of the would-be self-chosen leaders better, freer from hysterical emotional decision?

Despite abandonment of "hell-fire" theologies, there is still a widespread, lurking belief in the "old Adam" theory of human motivation. Too often the assumption is made that many, if not most, human desires are unworthy. Many a politician makes this assumption and refuses to trust voters with the true story which lies back of his decisions. Most advertisers, too, play upon questionable motives to sell cigarettes, soaps, or soup. The creators of high policy are often afraid to trust their nobler proposals to be accepted on the ground of nobility. These must be disguised by a false face of ugly, unideal motives. When the President of the United States wished to persuade the American people to spend billions of dollars to rehabilitate war-torn peoples and to raise standards of living in underdeveloped nations, he dared not present the idea as a mere humanitarian move. He felt it necessary to "sell" the proposal as a bulwark against the spread of communism. He assumed that fear would work where generosity would fail. Perhaps he was only realistic—in view of the probability that a mass appeal as such usually fails to uncover the better inner motives of men.

Many religious leaders insist that they must contend with an essentially evil human nature. Since, in their view, all men are by nature wicked, these bad impulses must be removed by external application of religious pressures. The "old Adam" can be exorcised by proper ritual, or by conversion, depending upon the beliefs of particular churches. In neither case are ordinary men thought to have a sufficient amount of good impulse to meet the challenges of life.

Or other religious leaders, more kindly disposed toward the possible goodness in their fellows, feel sure that this can be pulled up from under many layers of evil only by vigorous efforts on the part of righteous, chosen leaders. Men and women, they insist, will be good only as a result of much and frequent exhortation. The sermon must end with a section given over to "motivating" people to do that which they know they ought to do. This point of view assumes that of course there is agreement upon the question of proper conduct. All that is missing, therefore, is determination and will power. And these supposedly can be whipped up by persuasive stimulators of enthusiasm.

Any objective worker with conflicting human situations must conclude that "good" people are not always in agreement. It is possible for two persons with apparently deep religious convictions to take opposite positions on an important matter. And neither will be able to convince the other because each is certain that God is on his side. The exhortation to be "good" will not succeed in changing men. We suggest that the ills of the human race are due less to lagging zeal than to honest uncertainty as to how righteous people should behave. The problem is to develop a method whereby men can discover the good will in themselves by discovering the best action in specific situations. This revelation comes out of a willingness to try out in day-by-day practice the generalized rule of righteousness. The motivation comes then, not from high-pressure exhortation, but from satisfaction in doing a job, a job which benefits both oneself and one's fellows.

Mixed Motives

Human motives are neither all good nor all bad. They are both. In childhood, impulses of both kinds are present, both those which parents and Sunday-school teachers approve and those which they condemn. By the time one becomes an adult old enough to take responsibility, the mixture of the admirable and the unhappy is clearly set. The problem is to encourage the one and discourage the other. Most men want to be better than they are no matter how much their actions and words seem to belie such a hope.

In most specific actions motives are thoroughly mixed. It is seldom that any of us can enjoy the luxury of a purely idealistic decision unsullied by selfish desires. In one project, a community council prevailed upon a well-to-do dairyman to lend a piece of property to be used for a playground. He had expressed deep concern for the welfare of children. Following a noble impulse he donated use of a piece of property on which he had originally planned to erect a milk-processing plant, continuing to pay taxes though he had no use of the land. Some condemnatory cynics pointed out that his business increased considerably as a result of his generosity. True.

But was there anything to be regretted in this outcome? To give credit to the dairyman for a pro-social impulse, even while calmly recognizing his personal gain, is to avoid the devastating attitude of superior virtue. None of us, least of all the community educator, is free from motives of personal aggrandizement. Our seeking of good in others is more successful if we accept, with cheerful realism, the fact of mixed motive, in ourselves and in others.

The Humble Good

A main reason for failing to recognize good motives in others lies in the astigmatism of the observer. Because the other fellow fails to conform to a preconceived pattern of virtue, his ethical impulse is condemned for admixtures of selfishness. We must continually remind ourselves that the decision or action which, to us, seems low on the scale of altruism may represent a tremendous leap forward to the person who achieved it. These humble evidences of good will are to be judged more by the individual's own standards than by some distant ideal of perfect goodness. The standard of virtue, against which the individual measures his own conduct, grows from humble beginnings.

If one does not seek perfect goodness in others unmixed with lesser motivations, if one does not try to force men into his own pattern, one can expect the good motives within men to become strong when properly encouraged. Again and again, students working in communities have been astounded to see good will emerge in the lives of unlikely people. A plumber and his wife decided to give up their evenings to conduct a recreation center for young people; a housewife who was frightened and fearful of Negroes came to trust and work with them as friends; a merchant found satisfaction in giving food anonymously to make neighborhood picnics possible. Neighbors joined together to clean up the house and person of a retired invalid schoolteacher who had lived in neglected squalor. They formed themselves into a permanent committee to care for her, despite her critical sharp tongue. Small and unimportant evidences of good will? Small but not unimportant. They represent the beginnings of growth toward more all-encompassing good will in action.

Good will is in people; it can be brought out and cultivated. The motive for better conduct can be found both in the individual and in the act of kindliness. Individuals working together for the common good find an increased motivation growing out of satisfaction in mutual help. Motivation for the good need not be externally applied like a poultice. It grows from within individuals in groups and from the deeds of decency they do.

Persuasion That Increases Freedom

How do you persuade people to do that which they ought to do? The answers to this question have been unsatisfactory because the methods of persuasion used were too often inappropriate to expanding freedom. In America we have run to extremes. The emphasis has been placed either upon winning over separate individuals as in religious conversion or upon mass pressure as in exhortation, propaganda, and advertising. The former falls short because it has little effect upon men's social functioning and obligations. A man's freedom is found, not in escape from his fellows, but in finding self-expression together with his fellows. The latter falls short because mass persuasion tends to reduce individuals to statistical units on a public opinion poll. Without doubt, mass releases of news and persuasion can be made which are more compatible with the development of self-motivated personalities. But the face-to-face meeting remains the heart of the process by which personalities mature for freedom.

The techniques of persuasion which we have thus far failed to exploit to full potential are those developed in small groups. Here men and women can learn to persuade themselves to do that which they ought to do, in response to a method of encouragement. A single group, meeting time after time, will not produce the spectacular results of either a religious revival or a high-powered campaign of persuasion. But it may produce permanent long-time results in maturing individuals to become capable of using their expanded freedom intelligently. Many groups meeting over the nation might well have eventual results beyond present prediction. For no man knows yet how a nation would act whose citizens had matured to the responsibility of ever-expanding freedom.

Group Atmosphere

The idea of group atmosphere or group climate has been gaining in psychological respectability. It is clear that human personality is a product of group experience. That men's behavior might shift with the social atmosphere in which they are immersed is a matter of more recent observation and even experiment. Certain groups tend to bring forth a response of unquestioning obedience coupled with irresponsible revolt in a few, while others tend toward a more mature achievement of judgment. Some seem to encourage antagonism and competition; others, cooperation. Or the atmosphere of any single group may shift with changes in meeting place, in persons attending, in attitude of members. In part, at least, and in organizations that allow for flexibility, it is possible to set up and modify the social climate in such a way as to affect the responses of all, including even those who attempt to control atmosphere.

The method of encouragement seeks to expand freedom by increasing the area within which the group will take responsibility. It seeks to persuade people to do that which they ought to do by encouraging them to help determine for themselves the things they ought to do. It allows self-persuasion, mutual persuasion, in the interaction of individuals within the group. This is accomplished by the conscious use of group atmosphere.

We do not know enough as yet about group functioning to predict which steps will yield desired results. It is probable also that no single prescription will produce the same atmosphere in all groups. Expectation of progress calls for experiment. But there are standards by which success or failure of experiment can be judged. Any evidence that people have been released from emotional preconceptions and can act with less blocking by prejudice is important. As a result of such freeing, discussion usually becomes more intelligently pertinent, and members of the group make proposals which imply an expanding good will and willingness to work for the common good. The observer of the group process who is trying to judge success or failure must be careful to avoid confusing his own preconceptions with intelligence and good will. Outcomes will seldom be those which he had anticipated in advance. But if he is sensitive to the growth needs of other people, he will be able to recognize the act that means emergence of intelligence and good will for the other members of the group. The observer, being a participant in a process of mutual persuasion, himself may be changed as others grow.

What steps can be taken to create a freedom-expanding group atmosphere? Here are some which have proved promising in experiment.

Influencing Atmosphere

The physical setting for a meeting is important in organizing the stage for a relaxed informality. Too often meetings take place in school buildings where the serrated ranks of seats permanently screwed to the floor tend to regiment thinking; or in church auditoriums, where stiff pews call for silent acquiescence to exhortation; or in public buildings where elderly dust and a combined odor of stale tobacco, floor oil, and human perspiration bespeak futility and political deals. Some more friendly place, a living room in a home, a committee room in church or Y.M.C.A., a cabin on the edge of town, may suggest the free atmosphere in which it is possible to unburden one's thoughts. Comfortable chairs arranged in a circle, a central table upon which one's papers and elbows can rest, an open fireplace—all have been solvents of formality. A crowded small room is better than a small group huddled in one corner of a huge room.

The sense of ease and friendliness can be further enhanced by the manner in which people are greeted and the meeting is conducted. A matter-of-fact, non-oratorical tone of voice, a tendency to ask questions and listen, a refusal to be worried by periods of thoughtful silence—all are helpful. The well-timed joke without personal barb will often relieve tension. Participation from those who have had little experience in voicing timid thoughts may be encouraged by giving the impression that the meeting is incomplete until all have had something to say. Many people do not begin to think independently until they think out loud. Much patience is required to encourage their first feeble flights of intelligence. The opinionated extroverts can sometimes be held in check by the gentle insistence that the meeting is open to all contributors, and all must be heard.

The method of encouragement calls for an active seeking out of all pertinent points of view and factions. The encouragement is not limited to those who need little, or to those whose contribution is likely to be orthodox. It assumes that a priceless contribution may sometimes be made by an unassuming, hesitant soul. The expectation of something unique appearing in meeting as a result of universal participation becomes part of the group atmosphere.

The atmosphere of informality which invites even the timid need not mean slipshod failure to accomplish anything. A meeting can be both businesslike and friendly. Or rather, it may seek a compromise between extremes either way. The chairman should call for an end to discussion when it seems that all significant contributions have been made. This decision demands skill in judgment, and there is no assurance that mistakes will not be made. The important matter is that those coming together get the impression that business marches along in the midst of freedom. Frustration is the by-product of meetings which never reach a conclusion. Discussion should jell in agreement and action as rapidly as a consensus can be reached.

A businesslike impression is left by limiting the length of each session of a group, particularly if consensus in agreement is slow to develop. Rather than prolong the disagreement to result in repetition of the same arguments over and over, it is better to postpone decision and take up the matter again next time. If a termination time is agreed upon in advance, those who seek attention by being overbusy are more likely to remain until the end.

Above all, a group atmosphere is sought which grows out of the calm assumption that intelligence and good will are present. This in spite of evidence to the contrary. This all the more when stupidity is present and fiery ill will interrupts the meeting. Such an unruffled assumption, even when lubricated by humor, will not immediately result in the desired reactions. In fact, no social atmosphere which runs contrary to previous habits can be expected to produce immediate success. This appears slowly after persistent efforts. Intelligence and good will lurk in the personalities of most people, to be released by the patient manner that welcomes them.

Who Determines Atmosphere?

Every person who is within the room during a meeting contributes to the resulting atmosphere. Even those who remain silent but smile or frown, or laugh, or maintain a mask of poker-faced impassivity—all affect the attitudes of others. Absent people or events which have occurred prior to the meeting may tend to set the stage also. But these are a little remote for immediate control. The important fact to note is that each person in a meeting makes some contribution to group atmosphere.

Without doubt the chairman or discussion leader is the most potent setter of the psychological stage. Not that his influence rests upon his ability to dominate the meeting. Rather, he is in the best position to develop friendly informality, to give opportunity to the timid, and otherwise to use the method of encouragement. But others present may make their lesser conscious contributions.

It is difficult for a community educator who is sure he knows how to create the "proper" group atmosphere to sit back and watch a less experienced chairman make mistakes. In the earlier stages of community growth, the educator may act as chairman until matters are well started. (His mistakes? They are more easily forgiven!) Whenever, in his role as self-effacing leader, he turns over chairman responsibility to someone else, he must seek other ways of influencing atmosphere. He holds in abeyance his suggestions for conduct of the meeting, making brief remarks mainly to affect atmosphere positively, the quip to relieve tension, the explanation of a confused point. He holds in abeyance his own opinion on the matter at hand until others have spoken. He may at times call for expression from those who have remained silent.

The community educator, as contributor to atmosphere, studies the personalities in the group, their idiosyncrasies and the roles they play. One person may be the idea-proposer, another "the devil's advocate," another the blocker of activity, another the irrelevant wisecracker. These roles tend to persist in meeting after meeting, but they are not fixed. A quiet and unobtrusive contribution to atmosphere can be made by talking over with individuals the roles they are playing to encourage them to shift in order to allow others to grow. Even a chairman who has been missing opportunities can be approached diplomatically to improve his functioning. If the community educator is sufficiently concerned with the process in the group and sufficiently tactful, he or any other objective participant can make a continuing contribution to group atmosphere. And he can also train in the art of objective self-observation.

Observation of oneself and fellows, even when objective, can be overdone, however. Psychiatrists have a condemnatory word for too much concern with one's own processes. They refer to contemplation of the umbilicum. The social intestines can be observed so persistently that love of observation replaces desire for action. Groups come together, meetings are held, in order to accomplish something. Men grow and change by taking responsibility for jobs that are worth the doing. The anatomy of the process needs to be studied, but in connection with action directed toward some worth-while goal.

Limitations

The would-be controller of atmosphere wields no unusual power. Fortunately for his ego, he never becomes God. His influence is, at best, only supplementary to many forces far beyond his control. The physical and emotional states of the members of any group, their hopes and fears, the disappointments and triumphs through which they have recently gone, the events reported in press or radio which have caught widespread attention—all these and more contribute to social atmosphere. The community educator may use all his best techniques, yet produce disappointing results. He operates best when he watches his opportunities to effect changes gradually. Some group climate will always be present. A self-conscious would-be manipulator of atmosphere must realize that his influence is but one factor in a complicated total of many forces.

Operating by "Feel"

In the early years of aviation, flyers boasted of controlling their planes "by the seat of their pants." That is, they operated their tricky craft by "feel." In the years that followed, a vast array of complicated navigational instruments were developed to take the guesswork out of air navigation. Competent aviators no longer fly by "feel."

Competent operators within the realm of group atmosphere still depend upon "feel" or "hunch." Perhaps this is an unhappy admission for anyone with scientific pretensions to make. The scientific spirit does, however, call for honest appraisal of present limitation, in order to allow progress toward greater objective accuracy. The instruments for measuring position or progress in difficult social situations are not yet available; we are not even sure which variables should be measured. So we observe people and situations carefully, try to form a judgment free from bias, and operate upon the "feel" of the atmosphere. Perhaps social navigation will never achieve the machinelike certainty of aerial navigation. It never should if we prize freedom.

The would-be influencer of social situations should remain humble. He operates in the midst of two basic limitations. He is only one of many factors contributing to atmosphere. Though his experience be tremendous, he must continue to work experimentally in each situation, often depending upon that semiconscious judgment known as "hunch" or "feel." He is an operator with uncertainty, because he depends upon the cooperative response of those with whom he operates.

CHANGING PEOPLE WITH THEIR HELP

How do you persuade people to do that which they ought to do? You do more than take advantage of the freedom that democracy grants to apply pressure. You attempt to enhance that freedom by bringing people in on the determination of that which they ought to do. Although mass persuasive methods can be found which are not inconsistent with the development of self-motivated people, the face-to-face meeting for discussion is preeminently the place in which people can refine their own best motives.

The setting of the stage, the creating of atmosphere for the group, is a high art on which the last word has not been spoken. Certainly no single list of recommendations will work for all groups or in the hands of all would-be leaders. Any suggestions we have offered must be salted with the flavoring of any particular group and of the personalities that compose it. Further, it would be arrogant to claim that any experience to date had explored anything but preliminary possibilities. The study of group processes and atmospheres is being undertaken by social psychologists. But it needs also the attention of the people involved. Skill in the use of those social atmospheres which will increase self-direction cannot be learned from a book. It comes only as a result of the thoughtful experiment of real experience.

CHAPTER VIII

The Problem of Conflict

CONTROVERSY is human. It grows from the infinite variety found among men, a variety which comes to flower only in the vigorous climate of freedom. But conflict often understandably alarms people of good will. When thousands or millions representing one point of view line up to struggle against another large faction, they may threaten to rip apart the complicated fabric of civilization.

Some solution to the problem of conflict is needed, but not one which reduces all to a dead level of acquiescent agreement. We should have no desire to eliminate conflict from human experience. We should hope only to see social conflict tamed, to find a method for resolving difference without destroying it.

Human conflict is inevitable; it is immortal. It would not disappear even if the population were reduced to one. For the last man would probably disagree with himself. Rather than seek sterile agreement, modern men should decide to live in the midst of difference of opinion. The discomfort of difference is another of the prices man must pay for freedom.

Controversy provides much of the color for life. Two people who agree in many matters may each warmly conclude that the other is most intelligent. But this satisfaction is sober-faced stuff compared with that which grows from agreement reached only after vigorous difference. Much of human motivation grows from conflict in the form of competition. Even the self-styled collective utopias of modern days have found it necessary to use a whip of rivalry, renamed socialist competition. They gain home conformity by pointing to the need to do better than their "capitalist" rivals.

The problem is to hold conflict within constructive limits. It should not reach such vituperative vigor that people are split into mutually exclusive or warring groups. A sufficient amount of agreement should be found to allow solution to problems, to allow progress. There is need to develop a method for disagreeing creatively. This is a difficult task. For controversy is more newsworthy than agreement. Destruction is more exciting than construction.

Conflict is all the more interesting because it is so frequently interpreted as struggle between the forces of righteousness and evil. These are usually personified to produce a cosmos and community filled with gods or heroes, pitted against devils or villains. The idea that conflicts might be based upon something so prosaic as misunderstanding or failure to define words escapes the simpleminded seeker for excitement. The tendency to discover champions of good and bad in controversy is almost universal in human emotional thinking.

Unfortunately the gatherers and purveyors of news have encouraged this human weakness. Instead of seeking to educate a reading and listening public to calm appraisal of difference, they have sought out and magnified minor disputes; they have inflated ordinary mortals to become objects of veneration or hate. Both press and radio have sought to sell their sensationalized interpretation of news more than they have sought to mature citizens to live with sanity in a time of increasing crisis.

Modern man needs to achieve the scientific sophistication of a universe free from heroes and villains. He needs to learn that, if there is blame for misfortune, all share it. If there is praise, he should be generous with it. If there is a job to be done, all must work together. This is an essential for man to live at peace with himself and his fellows in a shrinking world.

Americans, in their great experiment with freedom, have demonstrated that they can forget condemnatory bickering and cooperate, but only under pressure of emergency. They have yet to learn how to resolve conflict, without destroying difference, in periods of relative calm when disputing factions are not forced to unite against some common enemy. They have yet to learn to differ in that creative fashion which solves problems while it matures disputants. Progress in the democratic experiment calls for widespread development of such ability. The small community is an important social unit in which to study methods for promoting such skill. The factional conflicts, the problems of representation of group interest, the frustration that grows from unresolved antagonism—all are to be found in microcosm in small community laboratories.

Constructive resolution of conflict is achieved mainly through creation and change of group atmospheres. It calls for skill on the part of a negotiator who makes conscious use of atmospheres. Community educators who must deal constantly with situations of conflict become amateur negotiators from whom professional conciliators might learn. The social atmosphere which proves useful in solving community conflict may prove equally valuable when applied to industrial or international disputes.

First Experience of Cooperation

Most small American communities are concentrated laboratories of conflict. The promoter of community welfare discovers soon that either inability to cooperate or the indifference of apathy threatens to block his most hopeful efforts. Of the two lamentable states, apathy is the more worrisome. Rival factions contending with each other at least pour out some energy, which might be redirected to better ends. Those who are apathetic have given up the struggle and can be stirred out of torpor only by great effort. Such social lethargy often comes, however, as a result of years of frustration created by fruitless conflict. The basic solution may lie in persuading people that they can make progress in solution of problems without losing their precious right to differ with one another.

When we enter a new community for the first time we expect to find rivalry among individuals and factions. Though we have been invited by one group, sometimes to further its own interests, our task is to seek out and bring all significant groups into the enterprise of growth. The dividing lines of conflict are multidimensional. They may be social, between the followers of one prominent feminine leader of society and another. They may be religious, in splits between rival churches or denominations. They may be industrial, political, racial, or even sexual, in a polite or none-too-polite warfare between men's and women's organizations. Sometimes conflicts are relatively mild and friendly, as between the Rotary Club and the Kiwanis. They may be bitter and even violent, as in contention between management and labor organization. They may involve grave misunderstanding growing out of lack of adequate contact, as in conflict between Negroes and whites or between native born and invading "foreigners." In exaggerated situations there may be fear and hatred openly expressed in fights and riots.

The idealizers of small-town rural America would often have us believe that the small town is the home of harmony. The external quietude can mask bitter factionalism. Or the smallness of the social unit reduces the dramatic character of conflict.

Whatever the contending factions, we conclude that our first task is to seek to persuade all to come together. Often those who have invited our help are dubious about our desire to include their rivals in a community council. But they go along in finger-crossed acquiescence as part of the price for our continued interest. We try to point out that all factions must be urged to join in the common enterprise lest an opposition be created by exclusion. There will be opposition in any case, as soon as a council which represents most groups deals with important controversial issues. The first step in learning community cooperation is the bringing together of all factions, whatever their previous rivalries, in a committee or council, to make progress toward some commonly desired goal.

Tension Reduction

As mutually suspicious groups come together, a deliberate attempt is made to create a tension-reducing atmosphere. To bring representatives of distrustful groups face to face in the same room is not enough. The result can easily be increased suspicion of each other unless some common interest can be found. The best focus of friendship is a mutually desired, active enterprise which can serve as a solvent of misunderstanding. But the social atmosphere is the surrounding medium in which the dissolving takes place, or fails to take place.

A tension-reducing atmosphere is encouraged by the open admission that tensions are present. This is stated with a cheerful lightness, rather than with the knitted brow of worry. It is stated with calm assurance that, although free people always will differ, they can find the common ground of good will. But differences are admitted openly and without alarm. There is a twofold purpose in the lightness of tone. First, it encourages expression of variety of opinion without fear of condemnation or of bitter personal attack. Second, it reduces the menace of self-righteousness on the part of contenders for attention. Nothing will increase tension as much as the participant in discussion who is so sure he is right that he can find no good will in the other fellow.

Cheerfully expressed difference is acceptable as background; the focus of attention is the job to be done. Contending points of view, vigorously expressed, can make for a lively meeting. But is progress made toward solution of the problem which brought the groups together? People grow in cooperative ability as they accomplish things together. Success for them is measured by the amount of action.

The problem chosen for first attention is preferably one whose solution is relatively free from controversy. This to prove that unity is possible even in the midst of difference. This to experience the satisfaction which comes from cooperative effort. In one small industrial city there was rivalry and a long history of mistrust between management and labor. When a planning commission was formed, we advised that both these factions be included, despite the fact that original initiative for organization had come from management. Both were represented from the first, along with various other contending rivals. There were numerous suspicious misgivings. Some progress toward greater understanding had been made over a period of three or four months, when a strike threatened to destroy the newly achieved unity. In the atmosphere of free admission of difference, the commission continued to meet. With determined cheerfulness they discussed, not the issue of the strike, but their common concern for community betterment.

One evening the planning commission met in the basement of a church one block away from the factory, in front of which a picket line marched. Previous meetings had taken place in the cafeteria of the factory. At this time the church had been deliberately chosen as neutral ground. Representatives of top management in the factory sat side by side with union officials to discuss a better system of garbage disposal! The light tone was difficult to maintain with a determined picket line near by. But progress in solution of the important problem of sanitation was made. Within ten days the strike was settled to the satisfaction of both sides. It would be difficult to prove that cooperative attitudes developed over garbage disposal had transferred to strike settlement. It would be easier to conclude that both factions had grown in ability to cooperate. With increased skill, even more controversial problems may in time be taken up with confidence that solutions can be found.

Consensus Versus Majority

The voluntary and amateur character of a community council forces it to experiment with democratic procedures at a more mature level than prevails in most legislative halls. There is no place for a triumphant majority and a disgruntled minority. There is no place for party-inspired opposition to fight to the bitter end for political advantage. There is no place for sensation-making, demagogic eloquence. There is place for the quiet attempt to find a consensus of all present before any action is taken.

During the as yet early stages of our experiment with freedom, we Americans have become much enamored of mere majority rule. At times we will even accept plurality rule when there is a choice amidst a more than twofold opposition. In any case there is always at least one unhappy minority which feels obligated to criticize or even block the program of those who were triumphant in the vote. Such a definition of democracy carried into a voluntary community council is unworkable. It leads to the attempt to quiet conflict by the coercion of a majority vote. Those whose voices were stilled by a too numerous opposition, and who remain unconvinced, can be expected to withdraw from the council.

The American Civil War established for all time that secession from the nation was not permissible—except that secession of refusal to take public responsibility. But individuals and organizations can secede from the democracy of a community council at any time. This unhappy fact is, however, more of a blessing than a curse, though the community catalyst will find it hard to convince himself of this when important factions start to walk out on the common effort.

There is no enforceable unity in a community council, no fixed membership. The unity comes as a voluntary choice on the part of members, based upon loyalty to projects which further the common interest. That is, actions undertaken must await the approval of practically all members. Those who fail to approve must be willing to give the proposed next step a trial even though they perhaps still harbor some doubts.

To those whose experience of democracy is limited to the open verbal warfare of irreconcilable oppositions, common agreement seems an impossible ideal. It is impossible as long as the group atmosphere calls for one point of view to triumph at the expense of all others. Consensus is possible in the group atmosphere which assumes it is possible. When a council has been so conducted as to convince members that no action will be taken which rides roughshod over the best impulses of anyone, then defensive and belligerent attitudes tend to disappear. Members of the group are more ready to address themselves to the problem at hand, less concerned to save face or play for attention. They are willing to take the time necessary to find an agreement which will command a near-100 per cent approval. The atmosphere sought is one of serious but kindly search for solution to the problem which all have admitted must be solved.

Creative Agreement

Does reliance upon consensus reduce a group's actions to a dead level of mediocrity? Is the least common denominator of agreement so low that the resulting action is unworthy of the effort? Not necessarily. For free discussion is a creative process. It may produce ideas undreamed of by participants before they came together. A free-ranging interchange of opinions conducted with the patient assurance that a constructive solution to difficulties can be found and in time will emerge frequently produces results in terms of both action and unity. The essence of the matter is that an atmosphere encouraging free expression of opinion prevail with the quiet confidence that major agreement will develop. Certain members of the group will emerge as radical proponents of action, others as reluctant conservatives. The rich variety of personal opinion assumes something other than a dead level of agreement, although it adds to the troubles of the community catalyst who tries to maintain unity in the midst of diversity. To hold the eager activists in some check while urging the uninformed and timid to new courage calls for skill that will tax the ablest community educator and add to his collection of gray hairs.

The search for creative agreement represents democratic action at a more mature level than the sensational, posturing belligerence of most political campaigns and many a legislative debate. That such a method is practical has been demonstrated by religious organizations, notably the Quakers, in conduct of business affairs and in social service projects. To achieve such a sophisticated level of behavior, people must forgo the joy of vituperative denunciation and the simple-minded naïveté to "point with pride" at one side of the argument while "viewing with alarm" the mistakes of the opposition.

THE ROLE OF THE CONCILIATOR

The tendency of men to regress to childish ways as they deal with conflict, even in a democracy, suggests the need for conciliators trained to raise social intercourse to a more adult level. The increased complication of modern life, the more serious consequences which flow from unresolved conflict seem to call for development of professional conciliators, skilled in the creative resolution of conflict, capable of helping antagonists to rise to a higher level of maturity.

In resolving intracommunity conflict, we have found a particular kind of mediation most useful. This is inherent in the role of the neutral counselor. When the winds of wild difference whirl about in a meeting, this conciliator represents the quiet epicenter of the noisy hurricane. Though he may often be accused by either protagonist of supporting the opposition, because he does not join in denunciation, he still represents a stable, calming influence.

The Neutral Counselor

What is the meaning of neutrality in the matter of resolving conflict? Neutrality does not mean colorless and craven agreement with everyone. Nor does it mean a retirement into an inconspicuous corner. The neutral conciliator is also a counselor. He has a positive function. He is neutral as to the currently raging conflict, but he is a partisan of progress: he presses quietly, often by his silent presence, for solution of problems at an ethically desirable level.

The neutral counselor is a director of social process through ability to affect atmosphere. If he knows his group and has persuaded them to have confidence in him, he becomes a symbol for good will and sane consideration of matters under discussion. A community catalyst who has deliberately faded into the background, to allow others to take the initiative, may make a contribution to greater objectivity simply by being physically present. If difference becomes vituperative, the catalyst may wish to surrender his self-effacing role for a limited time in order to take a more consciously participative part in solution of conflict.

In doing this, and throughout the discussions of the group, the successful conciliator must remain free from involvement in controversy, uncommitted to any proposed solution to problems. Situations of conflict and deadlock call for someone who can remain above the battle, able to listen with a friendly and judicious ear to all sides. Any representative on a community council who seems to speak for his personal interest or the advantage of his organization is immediately dismissed as a possible conciliator. A businessman with wide experience in community leadership points out that a merchant who buys from or sells to those he might offend in a meeting is immediately suspect. Better to have someone whose business success or salary will not be affected by decisions of the council. Representatives of all interests must be present, but there should be at least one person whose neutrality on conflict can tend to point the atmosphere toward good will.

The Technique of Agreement

When controversy becomes hottest, there is a method for working through to agreement. This calls for a skilled neutral counselor to be in charge of discussions until harmony has been restored. It depends upon carefully timed use of social atmosphere.

The particular type of atmosphere cultivated is known among psychologists as "permissive." Any community educator seeks to have discussion take place in a setting of emotional ease which readily accepts all points of view, even those which seem atrocious. The technique of agreement, however, works for and uses a permissive atmosphere in a rather specialized sense.

When a conciliator becomes aware that tension in conflict is piling up and threatens to break into verbal attack and name calling, he may deliberately set the stage to allow the outburst to come forth, by creating an impression of "non-shockability." Nothing that anyone says will create major offense or unseat the fundamental purposes of the group. This setting can be achieved in such a way as to invite emotional release.

The emotional outpouring which comes in a permissive atmosphere in the midst of conflict is known as a "catharsis." It is an unloading, a clearing out of social poisons and personal hates. It has been found that after the release of pent-up emotional tension it is often possible to move on to constructive steps which formerly seemed impossible. After catharsis, a remarkable change often takes place in the attitude of the speaker to whom release has come. He becomes apologetic for his excesses, wishes to make amends, may be eager to push on to the next steps which his former opposition had blocked.

The deliberate use of catharsis in a social situation is a process fraught with hazards. It proved itself first in counseling experience where a single patient in difficulty conferred with a psychologist. The latter could control the atmosphere and, more particularly, his own attitude. He could, as a result of training and experience, remain unshocked, to allow the process to work toward the emergence of rational good will.

When catharsis takes place in a larger group, it is much more difficult to be sure of the probable attitudes and responses of the numerous other people present, of those who are already irritated at the individual who is unloading his emotions. It is extremely easy for the permissive atmosphere to slip into attitudes of boredom, of anger and the tendency to retaliate, of indignation and the desire to walk out of the meeting. With an inappropriate response to catharsis on the part of others in the meeting, the group may break into frustrated fragments. The individual seeking cathartic release may become so enamored of his own eloquence that he develops into a perpetual complainer. Or the whole group may suffer an unpleasant episode without constructive result.

Skill on the part of the conciliator as social operator is the most important factor in bringing about a favorable outcome. He should be able to "sense" the reactions of people in the group, to balance the good of the release achieved by one person or faction against the amount of fear or indignation developed in reaction. He must be able to judge when a catharsis has about run its course and discussion can be redirected toward the constructive phases. He should be able to recognize when tension is building up toward an emotional outburst and must decide whether to allow an open display of pent-up feelings or to attempt to warn protagonists to remain silent, whether to seek a catharsis in a smaller subgroup whose members have attitudes which are more surely predictable. Unfortunately, it is not possible to give any formula for achieving such sensitivity to the thoughts and feelings of others except wide experience tempered by cool analysis.

In the early organizational phases of one community council a major tension developed between Negro and white members. The former came to meetings full of frustration and long-controlled indignation, hoping to have opportunity to blow off emotional steam about the discriminations from which they suffered. The latter professed themselves ignorant of such matters. Some became defensive at the implication that they or their friends were responsible for injustice; others became bored by repetition. Some were frightened away by implied threat to the sanctity of things-as-they-are; others were stirred to want to do something helpful. The problem, not unusual in situations of conflict, was to allow the disadvantaged minority sufficient catharsis to keep them in the council without frightening away the privileged majority who were being educated.

The conciliator attempted to remain a neutral counselor, interpreting one faction to the other. He allowed discussions to continue monthly over a period of a year before suggesting that any definite organization be set up. He tried to encourage a certain amount of time for the Negroes to express grievance at each meeting and some time for others to discuss and absorb this information. He conferred with the spokesman for the Negroes, advising him on how fast it was wise to move. He conferred also with white groups, appealing to them to accept with understanding patience. Finally, he tried with patient humor to continue a permissive atmosphere. This tactic succeeded in time. A strong council emerged. Several organizations withdrew their representatives in the process, however. The door was left open for them, and one or two returned when activities began to command respectful publicity. It is confidently expected that others will be gradually won back as the interest in public service projects grows.

The Capacity for Suffering

The wise conciliator is one who realizes that he may become the victim of personal attack sometime during negotiations. When the emotional outburst of catharsis comes, he may well be the target of the heated blast. Or his motives and actions may be subject to gossiplike misinterpretation, in meeting or in back-biting conversation in community. People change from long-held opinions only reluctantly and painfully. They may find it necessary to get rid of accumulated resentments by heaping them upon some convenient person in a prominent position. Or they may relieve the pain of change by attacking the person who, by his presence and word, presses for rational cooperation.

Such an attack places the neutral counselor in a peculiar position. He should remain "above the battle," but he must also be sensitive enough to the reactions of others to feel their pain. He must not become self-virtuous with indifference or wear the long-suffering countenance of the conscious martyr. Perhaps the best course for the conciliator is to accept the condemnations without resentment, to admit whatever truth there is in the comments (there is usually some truth—which of us mortals is free from legitimate criticism?), and to apologize for failings. It is possible then to go on to steps of improvement along with other members of the group. The conciliator must remain human in weaknesses similar to those exhibited by others, and in capacity for suffering.

One of the most successful international conciliators of modern times, Ralph Bunche, was peculiarly qualified for his task. As a Negro, he carried around with him, in the pigmentation of his skin, the evidence of his own and his people's suffering. He could succeed in negotiating situations of conflict which a man coming from a more privileged position would have had much more difficulty in handling. The "Suffering Servant" of Biblical teaching is a practical man of the world when helping to resolve the conflicts of men.

The Problem of the Spokesman

One problem common to all contemporary democracy adds to the grief of the conciliator. This is the peculiar behavior of the representative who feels he must speak for the organization which chose him. The reconciliation of differing points of view is much easier when each member of a group speaks mainly for himself and need not apologize for the sins of those who sent him. But when the member present is conscious of his role as spokesman for a whole organization, he loses some of his personal autonomy. He often feels under obligation to be more nasty, less cooperative, than he would be as an individual. He is reluctant to change his point of view lest he move away from the constituents who chose him, or lest he lose status with them.

There is no easy solution for this dilemma in community or in nation. Any answer must be only partial. The difficulty can be alleviated a little if the representative will report back frequently to his organization and call for instructions, thereby tending to pass along the education he is receiving in contact with other factions. Gradually, too, we have seen both representatives and their parent organizations move away from their own narrow interests toward a broader enthusiasm for community betterment. This is a slow process which calls for patient guidance by a conciliator who has faith in people.

When Agreement Fails

Sometimes in spite of the best of skill, or on account of its lack, the technique of agreement fails. A council disintegrates from apathy or breaks into angry particles. Then what?

Never give up! Such advice is hardheaded realism, not starry-eyed idealism. For human beings can be reconciled, provided some conciliator-promoter thinks the promised outcome worth the patient effort. It should be hastily admitted that the mortality rate among community councils is distressingly high, owing to a variety of causes found in difficult situations, difficult people, and confused conciliators.

When disaster befalls a council, wisdom may call for a temporary cessation of the organization in favor of a quiet talking over of problems and ideas by individuals. Eventually the time will arrive when some over-all discussing and planning body can be set up again. "Never give up" may include periods when to all outward appearances the council is moribund and its promoters have quit. If wise, they will bide their time with quiet conversation until the situation ripens for the next try.

BEYOND THE COMMUNITY

Methods developed in the microcosm of the small community have applicability to conflict in other social situations. Disputes between larger groups of men on more extensive historic arenas may have more ominous outcomes if allowed to continue without resolution. But human beings are human in large social situations or small. Perhaps they will give similar responses even though the chasms that divide them are deep and the consequences of failure to agree are disastrous to all society.

Professional conciliators have begun to emerge upon the scene of history. Their competence is usually assumed to be limited to some particular field such as labor-management conflict. Industrial mediators have been developed both in government agencies and among private citizens who are trusted by both disputants. Mediators of international discord have been slower to appear. And though they have some genuine success to report, their efforts tend to be limited to the lesser problems. So far the major issues that divide humanity into warring camps have been entrusted to conciliators only with great reluctance. Possibly this fear of trusting world-shaking questions to processes of reconciliation lies in the fact that international negotiations are carried on by governments that rest upon the pyrotechnics of legislative disputation.

Few conciliators have arisen to develop a technique of agreement for lawmaking bodies. It is doubtful that such people would be welcome if they offered their services. In political matters we human beings seem to shun the less spectacular methods by which agreement can be reached, preferring the heady excitement of battle, either verbal or physical.

Where conciliators have been successful in industrial or international disputes, it is frequently assumed that the good operator is one who can dream up a "formula," a compromise which both sides in conflict can adopt without loss of face. This notion stands in sharp contrast to the idea of the neutral counselor. The latter does not present his solution; rather he sets the stage for the disputants to discover their own compromise as they mature in a process of agreement. The conciliator as inventor-of-a-formula is a useful person who will continue to avoid much heartache for many people. But he tends to leave those he has rescued from their own stubbornness and stupidity as immature as they were before he went to work.

The method followed by the neutral counselor deliberately seeks to mature people by helping them to grow through conflict to agreement.

The Menace of the Righteous

A particularly obstinate type of inflexibility may block the way to agreement in international negotiations. This is the tendency for each of the disputant nations to insist that all virtue is resident in its position. And since God or the logic of history supports "our" cause, then of course no compromise is possible.

This self-righteous refusal to search for a common ground of good will with an antagonist is not limited to international disputes. It merely reaches superheated form when representatives speak for a nation. It can be found in disputes of lesser significance and lesser dramatic quality, in industry, in community. Wherever disputants can convince themselves that they speak as representatives of unchallengeable righteousness, the inflexibility appears.

Part of the difficulty may be made clear by considering the low repute in which the idea of compromise is held by certain people. Many high-minded folk insist that though an occasional compromise is necessary as a concession to the low political morality of men such opportunism calls for shamefaced apology, that pure ideals have been violated by unlovely expediency. A little successful experience in reaching agreement in the midst of community conflict will tend to convince an observer that creative compromise represents as noble an ideal as any "righteous" proposal brought into a meeting by participants.

The same point of view could be carried from community to the council chambers of international negotiators. Perhaps conflict between nations will be carried on with less self-righteousness when more citizens at community grass roots have had the experience of creative compromise. Representatives of nations will continue to speak as the inflexible emissaries of Deity until those at home demand that they become more human. If one day the human race destroys a considerable portion of itself in atomic war, a large portion of the blame can be laid at the door of those who were so "sure" they were right that they could not compromise.

Why Conciliation Fails

Other reasons for the failure of negotiation can be found in addition to the inflexibility of the righteous. Failure does not occur as often as the impatient would insist. The technique of agreement, by its very nature, is a slow process. Those who look for immediate or miraculous results often conclude that compromise is impossible and therefore there is no hope.

Conciliations fails many a time because it is never attempted. Factions in conflict remain apart, never meet each other face to face, but continue to make derogatory statements about the opposition. They point out that compromise with such unfortunate characters is impossible, thus proving (to their own satisfaction) that compromise is impossible.

Or conciliation fails because the meeting together is far too brief. Factions which do not ordinarily associate come into the same room long enough to present their "unalterable" demands, snarl at each other, and depart. This type of brief contact is to be found in labor-management negotiations much too often. Each camp meets to observe the uncooperative demeanor of the opposition; each issues a condemnatory statement to the press; each goes home to wait for impatience or public condemnation to force the opposition to yield. Conciliation has failed again because it has not been tried.

The bargaining or "horse-trading" session is not true conciliation. Most publicly observed negotiation is of this type. Factions come to the discussion with demands greater than they expect to achieve in the final settlement. They are prepared to yield a few points if the other side will do the same. It is this type of negotiation which has helped give a bad name to compromise. The final agreement is far from creative. It is rather an unhappy but workable cross between selfish desires of mutually distrusting antagonists.

Inadequate as horse trading is, it can represent the beginning of growth toward mature ability to differ and agree. Even though the attitudes be uncooperative, at least people are meeting in the same room, talking together, learning to adjust to each other's peculiarities. If they will continue to meet, even to bargain for selfish advantage, they may grow in mutual understanding and respect.

Secrecy in Negotiation

The advocates of political morality have often called for "open agreements, openly arrived at." This demand is presented as an antidote to the cynical and secret deals which have been a potent cause for war and basis for imperialism in the past. It is doubtful, however, whether the proposed cure is an improvement on the disease.

Theoretically, and for a mature democratic people, disputes should have public airing. Each step of the process by which agreement is reached should be objectively reported. But in the present state of immature sensation seeking, encouraged by press and radio, which refuse to accept responsibility for citizen growth, some secrecy in negotiation of most controversial issues seems imperative. Be it said in sorrow, most people are not adult enough to learn of vigorous controversy at second hand. And spokesmen for rival interests play to unseen galleries rather than address themselves to the creative solution of problems. Too frequently detailed reporting by those trained to find antagonism picturesque, results in an exaggeration of conflict, not in its diminution.

When participation in controversial discussion has become common, when men have had experience in resolution of local conflict, then they will begin to discount overexaggerated reporting of dispute in negotiation. Maturity develops initially in direct, firsthand experience. It can be extended later to secondhand experience, especially when interpretation of international controversy has been sensational and out of focus.

Neither complete openness nor extreme secrecy seems to be the answer to the ills of negotiation. The answer must be one which is made after much experiment and revised as experience matures ordinary citizens. Careful records of all discussion and agreements might be kept for endorsement by members of groups for whom negotiators speak. The freedom of the parent group to accept or reject an agreement by negotiators is important. This forces the spokesman-negotiator to report back to supporters and keeps him subject to their discipline. At the same time, freedom from minute-by-minute scrutiny of reporters allows them to act like decently motivated human beings. This is the main reason for experimenting with amounts and kinds of closed sessions in negotiation, to create the atmosphere which will allow men to discover their own best.

Men's conflicts can be resolved without destroying their differences. In seeking agreement, the big virtue is patience to allow men to find their own common denominator of good will. Educational processes are slow. When the thrills of spectacular rivalry and denunciation are to be abandoned in favor of the quieter but deeper satisfactions of constructive understanding, the educational process must be especially slow.

The achievement of a realistic patience will call for prodigious educational growth on the part of sensation-loving Americans. Most community educators will find it necessary to start with themselves in cultivating this virtue. Thereafter, members of community councils and committees will need to develop that faith in their own ability to solve problems upon which patience is based. Finally, the community at large must come to understand the slow processes by which agreement is reached. Critical voices which make sneering remarks about useless debating societies or "idle chatter" in meetings have yet to learn of the constructive functions of free conversation. Cultivation of the patience to work and wait for democratic processes to produce results is a major responsibility of the community educator.

Constructive Neutrality

It has long been assumed that those who wish to push for peace and progress among men must become vigorous advocates of some hopeful reform. There is every place for such individuals in a free society. And dull indeed is the community or nation which does not possess a few human gadflies. But perhaps the complicated times cry out even more for another contributor to progress, the conciliator. Those who have personality qualifications to become neutral counselors, those who are willing to train themselves in the necessary but difficult skills will undoubtedly always remain a minority in any population. It is possible to ask whether a constructive neutrality which encourages rivals to disagree creatively may not contribute more to peace and progress than many an advocate of even obviously righteous causes. Conflict-ridden communities present an ideal training ground for neutral counselors.

In an age when travel and commerce have sharply reduced the size of the world the human race has increased its tendency to divide into irreconcilable rival camps. It erects barriers to replace the now departed natural boundaries that separated man from man. All men of good will agree that these man-made barriers must be removed, even while they build them higher. Can the methods of agreement developed at the community level be adapted to larger and more dangerous quarrels? In our present state of ignorance it would be naïve to predict success for any method of resolving international conflict. The technique and philosophy which have succeeded on the small community scale are worthy of a tryout on the largest and most frightening problems. Unless some way is discovered for resolving these most basic conflicts, perhaps there will be no nations or civilization or communities as we now know them in which to seek for a common denominator of good will.

Participative Public Relations

ALL intelligent choosing must be based upon the availability of reliable information. Responsible citizens of a workable democracy must have a constant supply of pertinent and differing views. This situation calls for objective observers and honest reporters. News purveyors are fallible like the rest of the human race. And they are subject to pressures from editors, owners, advertisers, and others; still, with all its faults and failings, the press of America probably comes as close to providing complete and uncontrolled news as any in a large modern nation.

Freedom to supply information implies freedom to seek converts. Information is seldom supplied to inform merely. The reporter usually expects to persuade as well.

Every program of public improvement seeks to obtain support through favorable publicity. But the public relations should be in harmony with the purposes of the program. Otherwise improper publicity may become an off-color tail wagging the dog of the entire effort.

Responsible Presentation of News

Every attempt to supply information is, of necessity, selective. Perhaps it is possible to tell the truth and nothing but the truth. But the whole truth: that is beyond human capability. Whether the reporter be a friend telling of personal experience, or a newspaperman rushing in a story before it is "scooped" by a rival, or a scholarly historian telling of the struggles of a dead past, the reporting must reflect the selective bias of the purveyor of information. Rather than claim complete, unprejudiced coverage of news, modern or ancient, the honest reporter should openly admit his bias, in order to allow the reader to grow in discriminating judgment.

The advocate of community improvement, like every other competitor for public attention, is a special pleader. He gives information, to be sure, but information which places his program in a favorable light. He hastens to cover up with pleasant stories when some unfavorable bit of news or interpretation appears. But if he does no more than sing the praises of the work with which he is associated, he has fallen far short of accepting a full social responsibility. He should have a greater obligation to the people he informs than to the activities he supports.

A reporter is an educator, for better or worse. A denial of responsibility does not remove the effects of his reporting. The information he supplies contributes to maturation or to continued childish reactions of readers and listeners. The reporter for a community improvement enterprise will time his news releases to gain maximum acceptance. He may withhold certain stories while conflicting negotiations are going forward. He wishes to gain support for his cause. But he should value the support of freely and intelligently choosing adults above that of an emotional mass who say "yes," they know not why.

The Public and People

Most public relations programs seem to be based upon two tacit assumptions: first, that there is some small minority with superior wisdom or motives; second, that there is a none-too-bright majority to be won over as converts. The public relations expert is convinced that he speaks for the superior minority. The public is assumed to be lethargic or even resistant, a faceless, voiceless accumulation of humanity. Such an amorphous mass can endorse or condemn. It cannot originate. To "educate the public" then means to gain support for the fashions, ideas, or enterprises chosen by some minority, not the cultivation of ability to create.

Such a limited view of public relations is encouraged by early, unsophisticated reactions to the new instruments of mass communication. A syndicated and narrowly owned press, radio, movie, and television are all new to the stage of history. Human beings play with these gadgets as with new toys, naïvely, with little attempt to discover their possibilities as contributors to maturity. Mature use of new technical devices will not be possible until public educators can learn to look beyond the "public" to find people.

Fundamental educational processes are found at their best in small groups where personalities can interact. Nonetheless, mass communication of information can contribute to or hinder these processes. The deliberations and activities, the triumphs and disappointments of face-to-face groups can be reported in such a way as to encourage others to gain the benefit of such experience. The news of good works and of growth in responsibility should be publicized. Often the good will created by the publicizing of a little altruism seems to outweigh the significance of the generous act itself, in the mind of the person who was generous.

The Dilemma of the "Do-Gooder"

Those who are overly conscious of their good works sometimes coyly object to publicity. There are two explanations, at the extremes of contradiction, which may be offered. Reporting of socially useful activity may be resisted because of the tendency to oversimplify or misinterpret. The wrong kind of publicity may modify or destroy the original purposes of the altruists. Therefore it is better to work on in silence. The other explanation rests on Emerson's assertion that the world will beat a path to the door of the person who makes a better mousetrap or sermon than anyone else. The "do-gooder" may hope to remain modestly anonymous until his undoubted merit causes him to be sought out by eager reporters. The difficulty is that in a modern day of competition for public attention many a worthy person or enterprise languishes unnoticed, like the unseen flower upon the desert air.

Let it be stated that any reporting of his activities will always seem to be an oversimplification or a stressing of "wrong" emphases to the "do-gooder." This is inevitable. Someone on the outside, observing a process, will always see it differently from the way the active participant sees it. And many most significant projects are not particularly newsworthy to the read-and-run citizen of a nervous era. The community educator must be content with something less than a full philosophic discourse in justification of his efforts.

The solution to the dilemma lies somewhere between refusal to publicize and the coy hope that some reporter will pursue. The first step is to do some job of service that is significant enough to be reported. The next is to keep in touch with professional purveyors of news to offer facts and interpretation as they see fit. The third step is to remain simple and to avoid preaching. Let the job and its significance stand on their own merit. If interpretation is called for, make it an understatement rather than one full of too much enthusiasm. Let others use the purple adjectives, if they wish.

No generous activity should be undertaken for purposes of publicity. The motives should remain good will and growth. The publicity will come if the altruism is genuine. The purpose is not a boosting of the ego for some "do-gooder." It is the persuasion of others to go and do likewise.

ACQUIESCENCE VERSUS INVOLVEMENT

The ordinary public relations expert is satisfied with results far short of those sought by a competent community educator. The former usually seeks a thoughtless agreement, an acquiescence. The latter should not be satisfied until he obtains active participation in an ongoing program. And since a 100 per cent involvement remains an ideal to be approached only, his publicity task is never-ending.

There are two interdependent phases to the public relations program for a community educator. The first is the spreading of information and interpretation about plans and activities to create a maximum of favorable understanding. The second is the involvement of a steadily increasing number of people in discussion planning and action. The first is incomplete without the second.

Good Will and the News

The development of attitudes favorable to community improvement calls for active cultivation of the purveyors of news. Despite all the critical comments that have been made about newspapermen, they are human. They exhibit the same good motives and frailties which beset other mortals. They may insist that tales of conflict and disaster gain attention. But even they can understand that good will can be good news.

A cordial friendship between reporter and community educator will broaden each, to the benefit of the public. As in all good educational processes the growth is mutual. The community educator needs to become tolerant of and look beyond the surface cynicism with which most reporters conceal their more noble aspirations. The reporter in time will become tolerant of the determined hopefulness of the educator, may even come to admire an optimism that produces results. The education of each goes on in friendship, in shared comment upon progress, not in any direct teaching.

In the intereducation of reporter and community educator, is it wise to include the reporter as a member of a planning council, or make him chairman of a publicity committee? This is a moot point and no one answer is applicable to all communities. There is the difficulty that the reporter feels first loyalty to the newspaper or radio station which employs him. This is quite proper, but it sometimes results in a demand that *all* the news be reported at once. For the phrase "all the news" translate: "the selection preferred by the news agency." The selection called for by the educational ends of the council may conflict with the demands of an editor. Better then if the reporter can remain somewhat apart, especially during the period when he is being educated to the broad social purposes of a community council.

Most reporters seem to prefer a position of objective appraisal of community betterment activities rather than open involvement and advocacy. On the whole this is good, since it allows them to cultivate a loyalty to pure truth if they are so minded. And friendship is still possible between friends who remain somewhat apart.

The task of the community educator is to make news worth reporting. The task of the reporter is to tell a story without personal bias. Good will becomes good news when it represents a genuine contribution to the public welfare, free from pious posturing. Real altruism is rare enough to catch public attention when it does appear. But the activity of service must be genuine. Newspapermen are quick to discover and discount any plausible stunt put on to catch their attention. It is better to carry on an altruistic action unrecognized for weeks or months than to gain approval for something false. A community council or group of students who will push ahead to do some job of self-giving, cheerfully and obviously enjoying the experience, will catch the interest of reporters and of the public. The news which the community educator helps make is actual action of cheerful good will.

Spreading the Participation

The immediate purpose of favorable publicity is the gaining of support for programs of social improvement. The longer-run purpose is the involvement of larger and larger numbers of persons in these programs. The publicity creates a community atmosphere favorable to wide participation. The publicity and the participation are complementary to each other.

A program of constructive altruism does not appear full grown like Minerva from the head of Jove. It starts with small beginnings and moves on to wider and wider circles of participation. Usually some small group develops the courage to pioneer in service, hoping that its example may prove contagious when properly reported. It is important that the group beginning altruistic action be sponsored by a community council or some other recognized organization—to avoid the accusation of being "queer."

Sometimes those who hear about a generous act on the part of other people protect their own uneasy consciences by concluding that such people are not normal. They "must" be strange pursuers of peculiar hobbies if not actually candidates for special mental care. It is important that altruism be kept within the range of normality. Those who indulge in generous acts for the general good should have acceptable sponsorship and should themselves work with human humor, avoiding better-than-thou attitudes. Above all, they must do the job because they enjoy it, not because they are hag-ridden by a driving conscience.

What kind of expression of good will is best as a start? The more it can deal with physical construction, resulting in aching muscles and callouses, the better. Physical activity can be photographed and described. This is an important point. But more important is the need to convince people that good will can pass beyond the stage of pious talk and hopeful wish. The reporting of a discussion and planning meeting is essential but does not yet represent vigorous action. The coming together of former rivals and the development of agreement is valuable but may still be largely verbal. The sight of people sweating together cheerfully to accomplish something for the benefit of all—this is dramatic.

News of financial gifts to worthy enterprises is carried regularly by the press, the larger benefactions receiving the bigger headlines. Financial support is certainly important, but it is an incomplete expression of active good will. The reading public has come to accept the gift of money as necessary to the support of many essential services but scarcely a unique expression of good will. There are many who will contribute of their wealth, but not of their time and energy. The true participation sought goes beyond financial interest to include dirt on the hands and aching muscles.

Good-will activities which stretch the muscles are not the only kind which are newsworthy. But in an era when men live on a heavy diet of words and when generosity is expressed mainly in financial terms, giving of time and energy in thoughtful participation is unusual. In the end, a combination of physical work, discussion, planning, and verbal statements makes up the content of news of good will.

Beyond the Pioneers

It is useless to create a community atmosphere favorable to participation in good-will activities unless some steps to utilize the atmosphere follow. It is discouraging for courageous pioneers to begin activity unless others are persuaded to do likewise.

Interpretation of good-will activities by newspaper and radio is followed by personal contact and conversation, by speechmaking, by invitations to people and organizations to join in expanding activities. The speechmaking needs special comment. A formal address to a huge audience which can be reported in the press is not as effective in follow-up as many discussion-conversations with more intimate groups. The speaker who orates with an eye upon the reporters in the audience lacks the spirit of friendly exchange between equals which is important for involvement in self-motivated activity. The purpose is to make it easy for an increasing circle of people to become active in planning and in work. This is best accomplished through personal contact with those who have become enthusiastic through participation.

The first leaders, the pioneers in good will, are likely to be those who have sensitive social consciences and some experience in work for the common good. Such people are usually overbusy before the activities proposed by a community council begin. They are best qualified because they are busy. The well-known excuse that one is interested but cannot take time for a proposed activity is sure evidence that the enthusiasm of conviction is lacking. These busy people who say they cannot find time frequently make up a community council initially. They are the people who take part in the first labor for the common good which becomes newsworthy.

Gradually, however, the circle widens. New personalities join the forces, some by spontaneous choice, but more through active recruitment by the convinced. The invitation to contribute time and talents, made in personal conversations and in small groups, is an organized part of a program of public relations. The finding of assignments for newly recruited people is as important as the creation of favorable attitudes by mass distribution of news.

The new active participants cannot be kept in an inferior position, subordinate to the original more experienced and more courageous few. They, too, must have the experience of participation in democratic planning. The initiators often find difficulty in retiring gracefully in order to give the others a chance at officerships and committee chairmanships in a council. The best solution is to cultivate the idea of rotation in responsibility, passing perhaps half of the jobs on to newcomers each year while half are held for more experienced individuals.

Fortunately, there is almost an infinite amount of opportunity for good will. No one need be denied his chance to join in the common effort to help other people. There is a limit only to the positions with high-sounding titles. The experience of rotation into and out of various functions makes possible the training of a constantly widening group of people. More and more participants learn that service to others provides satisfactions which are found in no other experience, that active good will is contagious and works best in a democratic atmosphere. Having been involved in projects which are reported as newsworthy, participants become sophisticated to discount or even resist inaccurate reporting of such events.

WORKING AND WAITING

A program of public relations is successful when it inspires eagerness to serve. If mere reluctant good will is the outcome, the effort has resulted in failure. If enthusiastic good will be the end sought, then there must be willingness to wait for this to develop. Lasting enthusiasm is not a quality which can be turned on or off by a skillful manipulator of publicity. Eagerness to serve may be cultivated in others by a judicious combination of the ability to work and the ability to wait.

When people take the initiative in service, they must be allowed to have the satisfaction of making their own decisions. When a person has decided upon some generous act, there is nothing which dulls the brightness of his decision quite as much as the urging to be generous. Give people time to be kind. Properly inspired and given time, they will come with ideas, money, offers of help, willingness to go to work. But they must be allowed to serve in their own way, according to their own choosing. Self-choice is the beginning of participation. The discipline of the choosing comes later as the involvement with others calls for group decision and group effort.

The process of working and waiting really works. With determined faith in people and in the processes by which they grow, results may be obtained which seem remarkable to the onlooker. Students, with the help of small local minorities, have been persuaded to gamble upon good will. They have worked on some project in the hope that their initiative, when sympathetically reported, would result in an imitative outflow of generosity. Seldom have they been disappointed in numerous experiments with publicized altruism.

An Experiment with Good-Will

A group of fifteen, including students and a faculty couple, took part in a voluntary summer work camp on a Caribbean island. During a brief period of eight weeks they undertook to construct a playground, including a concrete platform for games. They had been invited to come by a local committee which had been formed at their suggestion but which gave little assurance of cooperation in the endeavor. The local tradition was antagonistic to physical labor, except for those who had to dirty their hands in order to live. Yet the section was so poor that little financial contribution could be expected. Local custom also called for a dependence upon distant government to carry to completion projects of public betterment, rather than a development of planning initiative at home. Would well-publicized generosity prove contagious and result in a spread of self-motivated participation?

The group went to work in the hot and tropical sun and deluging rain, hauling sand and gravel. The local press was generous in reporting such an unusual event as Americans' abandoning the comforts of their homes to live and work in primitive circumstances. Many came to see; others learned of the endeavor with feelings ranging from incredulity, to suspicion of such "queer" antics, to admiration. Questions were raised as to whether there was not some "catch" in the enterprise, some benefit to be gained by some persons or institution. Attentive wonderment increased when it became apparent that the group was unsponsored except by a college intent upon studying processes of community growth, that no religious sect was seeking expansion through converts as a result of the work. To all inquiries the group insisted that their work was nonpartisan, nonsectarian, and sought to bring together all people and factions willing to work for the common good.

Four weeks of hard labor were necessary to convince the unbelievers that the enterprise represented bona fide generosity on the part of normal human beings. By then it became apparent that the project would not be completed if help from local residents were not made available. Trucks to haul materials, sacks of cement, lumber were necessary. In a sense the group threw itself upon the generosity of citizens of the island to make possible a development to benefit themselves. Students labored, sweated, and complained. All of them were normal young people, free from pious postures. They were willing to work but were not at all sure that their efforts would be rewarded with understanding and the kind of support that would allow them to complete their task.

The triumph of participative support was all the more dramatic to them when it did come, in view of their earlier complaining doubts. The convincement of an educational process was great when they discovered that the generosity they had demonstrated was contagious.

After four weeks of labor, punctuated by a few visits to influential citizens and clubs, the tide of generosity began to flow. The group and the project were "adopted" by two service clubs located in near-by small cities. These, in friendly rivalry, sent trucks to haul donated sand and gravel and raised money for cement. The mayors of the two municipalities gave cement, and one sent a truck and crew of men to help. Contributions came from several interested individuals, some as a result of solicitation, some spontaneously. Machinery and tools were loaned by Presbyterians, Episcopalians, the Church of the Brethren, Methodists, Catholics, and government agencies.

One unhappy situation yielded to the solvent of active good will. For years there had been misunderstanding between Catholics and Episcopalians, centering in the persons of a priest and clergyman of the respective faiths. These two (though there were unpleasant stories of enmity between them) had never met each other. Convinced finally of the nonsectarian character of the work, they both came to labor with the group. They were introduced to each other for the first time. They worked with the students, at first on separate days, each with full knowledge of the other's participation. At long last, they worked together on the same day with full pleasure in the experience. On the last day of the project, each of the men separately thanked members of the group for having overcome the misunderstanding and made them friends. This, they insisted, was a friendship which would last. Said one, "If you accomplished nothing more this summer, this bringing of us together was enough to justify your whole effort."

One episode loomed large in student thinking because of its dramatic demonstration of the contagion of good will. For several days the group had worked at the pouring of concrete with a wary eye upon a dwindling supply of sacks of cement. More had been promised by several people who were beginning to demonstrate generous impulses. But the cement on hand diminished and no more appeared. Finally came the day when it was announced in tragic tones that there would be only enough left to allow half a day's work for the following day. With true appreciation of the dramatic the students suggested that they might as well quit since their efforts were so poorly appreciated. They were urged to work at their usual pace while a faculty member took the bus to the near-by town to see what could be done in the emergency. He found none of the promisers of aid available but spread about the story of the emergency. He returned that evening to the group with empty hands and only the assurances of blind faith.

At ten o'clock the following morning a truckload of cement arrived together with the president of the municipal assembly of the near-by town. Faith had been vindicated in an almost miraculous fashion. And the students marveled openly. Be it said, however, that this sort of miracle cannot be predicted and the wait for one to happen can be wearing on the nerves. The gratification when one does take place is enough to overcome several episodes of disappointment. And the miraculous expression of generosity happens much more often than is thought possible by those who dare not risk a gamble with good will.

It might be pointed out also that good will sometimes needs

the prodding of publicity. People wanted to be generous, but the acuteness of an emergency had to be drawn to their attention.

The flow of generosity rose in volume throughout the eight weeks. It included gifts of bananas and coffee from neighbors who had little to give; it included food and reduced prices on purchases from merchants; it included invitations to dinners and week ends at the expense of individuals and government agencies. But the ultimate proof of growth lies not in gifts but in willingness to accept responsibility.

The people benefiting most immediately from the project were unused to cooperative effort for the general good. They lived, not in a town or settlement, but out on the hillsides in an individualistic existence in a forest-coffee economy. They came together in common effort for the first time, with the group of students. Gradually the number of hours they spent in physical labor on the project increased, over the summer. By the end of the period they had made their spontaneous decision for the future. A group from the college must return another summer and help them build a small school. Over the year, they would make arrangements for construction, collect wood and money to be used, and set aside a month or more out of busy lives to work with the students on the job of construction. This was their decision and their acceptance of responsibility. Some will fail to live up to their promises, but the planning represents a major step toward participative responsibility.

More distant helpers were not to be outdone. Service clubs and public officials of the near-by towns formed committees to join in the planning for the future. They accepted the plans for the school and began investigating a housing project in another valley as an activity for a second work camp in the ensuing year. Having succeeded in raising money and in providing tools and equipment, they undertook to finance the expanded program.

Plans for the Future

The ultimate proof of success in participative public relations is found in the behavior of the newly inspired participants. The proof was unmistakable in this experiment with good will. Dwellers on the island took the initiative to plan for the succeeding summer. The local people in the valley of our endeavors were too poor and inexperienced to make plans alone. The great outflow of planning energy came from their friends of near-by towns, people higher on the scale of wealth and education. These raised money for continued summer operations, made contacts with government offices, interested high officials, helped to obtain loans of cars, trucks, and other equipment, and met with local committees to plan details of further labors. It is well that these people did so, since both the distance of the College from the actual scene and the language difficulty made planning from the continental United States laborious. The initiative rapidly passed from the College to the citizens. The College reached the point of merely agreeing with proposals made.

The uniting of efforts in planning by peasantlike farm people and upper-middle-class folk made continuing work possible. But it also represented a cooperation between classes unusual in the particular social setting in which we were working. Perhaps this is one of the kinds of cooperative efforts between ordinarily separated classes that needs to be explored by those who are interested in improving the lot of the underprivileged in underdeveloped sections of the world.

The end is not yet. This is another of the situations in which success is discovered in the fact that an ongoing chain reaction is started. A successful experiment in good will is one which is continuing.

Active good will, well publicized without preaching, tends to produce increasing amounts of initiative for more good will. The process is an ongoing chain reaction. But it requires patience, the willingness to wait until the contagion of altruism has a chance to infect other people. People will come to a project of genuine good will with offers of help, if given a chance. They can be stimulated, even prodded, by favorable publicity, by unsalesmanlike personal contact. For growth, they never should be forced.

The Work Camp as Advertising

The work camp is a prime example of a good-will activity, dramatic enough, sincere enough, laborious enough to command favorable publicity. Often the actual job completed is less important than the idea of self-help spread, the spirit of generous service unleashed, the friendly understanding achieved. We have had heads of institutions appeal to us for help from student work camps to construct some necessary building or carry on some needed repairs, all at a financial saving to the institution. We have often refused, taking the position that it is not our function to supply cheap labor even for a worthy cause. Rather our responsibility is to spread good will and understanding, a problem in creative public relations.

In order to make a work camp an example of participative public relations, it should involve local people in the planning from the outset. We object to going into a situation of need on the plans of the central office of some church or social agency merely. Local citizens must want us to come, be prepared to take at least a minor part in activities, and hold out the hope that they may increase the amount of their participation and responsibility.

The work camp which brought such generous response met these conditions. Our local collaborators were eager to have the students come but were quite unsure about their own functions and responsibilities. They were eager but hesitant, a handicap which wore away with the weeks of the summer. We learned later that curious folk, government officials, citizens from neighboring towns, newspaper reporters, and others had visited the scene of our activity during the first four weeks of unrewarding labor. Unknown to us they consulted with our participant collaborating friends. The enthusiastic endorsement which the students received in these conversations behind their backs was a chief contributor to the later outflow of generous support. The advertising of good will by convinced word of mouth is a major form of publicity which cannot be bought. A full newspaper and radio coverage of the activity would prove less than effective unless the conviction that good will was sincere could spread out in concentric circles from the activity.

This work camp, like many another in an underprivileged part of the world, suffered from lack of tools and materials with which to work. Students sometimes complain when these essentials for the accomplishment of the job are slow in arriving. With characteristic American impatience, they do not wish to waste time waiting for the slower pace of another culture to provide supplies. It takes some time for them to understand the educational process by which citizens of any culture learn to take responsibility. Eventually the tools and materials were made available but only after days of wondering and worry. The pain of uncertainty was part of the process by which students learn how good-will responsibility spreads.

When technical assistance programs go forth to so-called under-developed parts of the world, they are frequently well financed and well equipped by governmental agency or foundation. If so, the workers sent out may be handicapped at an important point. They are so well prepared materially that they do not need to call upon local people to open their reserves of good will. The fact that the student work campers had to throw themselves upon the generosity of those they had come to help made both public service and self-help contagious. The possibility of using the generous but amateur impulses of young people to stimulate an out-pouring of cooperation among those who need to learn self-help is one which might well be examined by agencies planning technical assistance work. Perhaps the generous amateur can supply an ingredient which no technical expert can find, no matter how well trained.

A major purpose of work camps is to let people know that certain needs exist, that something can be done about these needs, that some otherwise normal people are willing to make sacrifices to attempt to meet the needs. The camp is an example of good will genuine enough to inspire favorable publicity.

Students as Advertisers

In service activities of a work camp nature students become favorable public relations influences. This is one of the points at which college and community can meet in a most positive relationship. Working young people can be advertisers of good will, but they also can encourage a favorable attitude toward the student generation, which is often condemned for thoughtless irresponsibility. The fact that they are cheerful, energetic, inexpert, and rush in where angels fear to tread makes them acceptable in many places where more sober people would be rejected.

By encouraging attitudes favorable to good will, working students create also favorable responses toward eager young people, toward education, and toward the college that sponsored them. Bumptious youthful energy can be turned toward useful purposes.

PATIENT FLEXIBILITY

There is no guarantee that good will in action will prove contagious. Each attempt to find altruism in others by this process is an experiment. Each attempt is a tryout of an idea, as much of life is an experiment in ideas that must be tested. The initiator of a generous activity must be prepared to be disappointed by a failure of response. Even more alarming, he must be prepared to modify his goals, his definitions of goodness, as more and more people participate. When people become genuinely generous, they do so in their own way, not according to some blueprint pre-prepared by some promoter of good will.

The sure-fire fixed response sought in most publicity is a matter quite alien to the flexible concept of good will sought by publicity for participation. The satisfaction gained is not that of executive-type efficiency in ordering predictable results. It is rather the greater satisfaction of seeing people do good things because they want to. If the promoter of altruism can be patient and will accept the good-will gestures of others as they come spontaneously, he stands a chance of being educated beyond his own limited concepts of the good.

CHAPTER X

The Democratization of Social Research

WHEN scientists, bent upon research, at length turned their attention to human beings, they encountered an unprecedented difficulty: the response of the material under investigation could materially alter the conclusions reached. Failure to cooperate with the researcher or open resentment against his efforts could easily cause him to form conclusions which were quite incorrect. When data could be collected without the subjects' being aware that they were under scrutiny, the results seemed most certain. But a people that trumpets its scientific sophistication in every newspaper Sunday supplement could not long be kept in ignorance of research activities which collected information about themselves.

The reactions of human material under scientific observation or experiment are not necessarily negative. They may cover a complete spectrum of attitude from violent resentment to prideful antics in appreciation of a supposed honor. The reactions tend to be extreme. Once the idea is accepted that trained observers are about to draw conclusions after data about oneself has been collected, it is difficult to remain indifferent. Those who tend to be resentful object to being reduced to the status of guinea pigs by some investigator who claims superiority in brains, training, or objectivity and who possibly seeks the power which self-chosen superiority may threaten. Those who feel honored by unaccustomed attention seem to be flattered by the selection of themselves or their community for study. The conclusions reached by the scientist are dependent in part upon the kind of welcome he receives.

These comments apply to the researcher-as-outsider. When he enters a community, he may seek to make himself a part of it as a "participant-observer." But even as he becomes a citizen like anyone else, he hopes, he may still be regarded as a creature apart, to be eyed with reserve. To reduce the variable effects of welcome to a minimum the subjects of observation, the participant-citizens, must themselves become part of the research.

To discover means for democratizing social research has been a major effort for our work in communities. We do not mean to disparage the work of highly placed and expert social scientists. There should be every encouragement for their elaborate and often expensive studies, as they collect fundamental data and develop important theory. Our concern is to make their findings available to and develop research skill in those who will use these as bases for action.

The ordinary citizen of a community, if he uses research at all, thinks of it as an aid to contemplated action. There is no reason for believing this point of view inconsistent with that of the "pure" scientist. The citizen can gain from theory if it can be presented in comprehensible and useful form. The scientist can learn from practical experience if he can gain the cooperative partnership of the citizen.

The method of action-research is peculiarly adapted to this democratic emphasis. In encouraging its use by ordinary citizens of ordinary communities, there will undoubtedly be some loss of the extreme and painful objectivity of the avowed social scientist. But there is a more than compensatory gain in the gradual increase of scientific objectivity of ordinary men.

When social research is democratized, the scientist comes down from his pedestal of learned aloofness; his subject rises from his abject role of material-under-observation. Together they observe, record, and experiment on the situation that affects both. Both become simultaneously experimenter and guinea pig.

THE ART OF SCIENTIFIC GUESSING

Certain embattled defenders of religious orthodoxy have condemned scientific thinking as a mere matter of "guesses strung together." Though the description was meant to be devastating, it actually is not too inaccurate. No scientist, possessed of the humbleness which should accompany competence, will do more than claim that his conclusions are tentative. They are the best guesses that can be made on the basis of all the presently available evidence. They are never finally fixed in authoritarian fashion but are subject to modification with new information or new philosophic interpretation.

It can be argued that all conclusions of the human mind are but guesses, some wild and wishfully unrelated to facts, others more cautiously thought out and based upon experimental testing. The laboratory scientist or systematic theorist may spend a lifetime of suspended judgment waiting for the careful collecting of evidence in order to approach ultimate truth more closely. The practical man living in the world of real affairs cannot afford the luxury of waiting to be finally right. He frequently is forced to act within a limited period of time, on the basis of whatever information is available, even though this be clearly inadequate. The uneasy distrust which separates man of affairs and scientist is partly to be explained by differences in the amount of time each can allow himself to arrive at a satisfactory conclusion. The time differential to each may often seem to be that between now and never.

When we attempt to democratize research, we are dealing with people in communities who may not regard themselves as men and women of affairs. Nonetheless, as they grow in leadership ability, they find themselves under the necessity of collecting facts in order to arrive at important decisions. They often find that adequate and complete information is not available in the limited time the situation or their patience will allow. They suffer from an ailment that assails all modern men, including the most profound scientist outside his own particular field of competence; the world is so complicated, and dependable information so uncertain, that they are forced to act upon their best guesses. The problem is not to replace guessing with unassailable thinking, based upon complete assembling of facts. The problem is to bring the guessing more in line with the best scientific thinking.

No man is free from the tendency to guess. It is impossible to approach any new situation or experience with a complete "know-nothing" attitude. Previous experience, reading, or thinking will cause the formation of certain attitudes or assumptions which must affect the approach to the new. The open mind does not mean one free from previous thought.

When we attempt to interpret the events and tensions of a meeting, we are indulging in scientific guessing. Our analysis of personalities and their actions becomes the determiner of our further actions and contributions to group growth. The guess is more nearly scientific if made in the light of known facts and if stated with conscious objectivity. It must be held as tentative, for no assumption can be considered infallible.

In attempting to encourage development of the art of scientific guessing in our collaborators, a first step is to make articulate (at least to ourselves) a few of our own guesses. Some of these are hypotheses for testing during limited time periods of work in communities. Some are part of the equipment of faith for a lifetime without which a worker with human beings is lost. All are subject to reexamination and modification with accumulating experiences.

Some Scientific Guesses

The seeming uncompromising firmness with which most of the following hypotheses are stated should not mislead. They are phrased positively in order to be clear, in order to provide a basis for the commentary of other observers of human processes.

Some of the principles which can be formulated from experiences to date are these:

The best place to study man is in his native habitat, the community where he lives.

Basic human processes are best observed in small community centers. These processes can perhaps then be applied to more complex social settings in larger agglomerations of men.

Permanent social changes come as a result of a process so slow as to be almost imperceptible at the time. Sudden, dramatic events are not to be regarded as evidence of real change unless they are episodes in the slower, less spectacular process.

There are certain fundamental human reactions almost universal in all men despite great differences in culture, language, and tradition. Which reactions are universal and which dependent upon local tradition is not clear as yet.

Even within a relatively homogeneous region, there are wide differences in community maturity or in community atmosphere. Maturity and atmosphere as used here are difficult to define, but they are very real to those who have attempted to work with more than one community.

The experience of cooperation begun with some simple and relatively uncontroversial project will often lead on spontaneously to larger and more inclusive endeavors; the limits are as yet unknown.

Ordinary people, as a result of working together, will evolve solutions to their own problems often superior to those proposed by experts.

Leadership is not necessarily found only in a favored few with "natural" ability. It can be discovered and trained in numerous people, many of whom are, at the beginning, seemingly unpromising.

Most people have undeveloped capacities for cooperation and intelligent good will which even they themselves do not suspect. By use of proper methods these can be released and harnessed to further the common good.

The process of talking-working-and-talking together, if pursued with patience and skill, will resolve apparently irreconcilable conflicts and allow unpredictable, constructive achievements to take place.

The community educator obtains maximum results, not by telling people what to believe or how to act, but by encouraging conditions which allow them to work things out for themselves.

Discounting Assumptions

Any catalogue of scientific guesses would inevitably be incomplete. The most important omission would be those conclusions about ourselves or about human nature which are accepted uncritically because of the civilization within which we live. Nonetheless, to bring a few preconceptions to the level of critical consciousness is clear gain.

The main purpose in making assumptions articulate is self-discipline. Scientific objectivity is not a happy state at which one arrives for all time. It calls for a constant struggle. A most important phase of that never-ending effort is the examination and reexamination of conclusions. The social scientist, as he enters into the partnership of shared research, needs especially this self-critical discounting of his own presuppositions. This is most essential for him in avoiding a fatal arrogance which will set him apart from his collaborators.

In attempting to fill the role of social scientist thus defined, we confess to these few assumptions as examples. Though the main motive be self-discipline, there is no objection to public confession. In general, we admit these, and we hope other, preconceptions to ourselves. We do not present them with knitted brow to our community collaborators. They will often be mentioned in a casual atmosphere and with humor as an aid to the achievement of similar self-discipline on the part of citizen co-operators in research.

Guessing of some sort is inevitable in all thought and action. When it is scientific, it has two useful functions: the guidance of continuing research and the providing of specific hypotheses for proof. In the first role, it is important that assumptions be held tentatively and that they be subject to constant critical reexamination with experience. In the second role, some guesses are reduced to clear-cut and manageable propositions which are provable by exact research methods. For ordinary mortals the first function is more important as contributor to men's stature in self-analytical objectivity.

THE ACHIEVEMENT OF COLLECTIVE OBJECTIVITY

A freedom from personal emotional involvement, an ability to see life as it is with cheerful detachment—these are important attitudes for modern man to acquire. They provide a mood which is friendly to the process by which man can help guide his own growth in a period of change. But we have encountered a fear of accepting the very attitudes that might free them on the part of certain students and citizens. The familiar fears are comfortable; the unfamiliar freedoms seem to threaten.

Fear of Objectivity

Most people can be objective about those matters which are remote from themselves. They can be objective to the point of boredom because they are not concerned. As they become a little more interested the mood of aloofness is more difficult to maintain. Interest frequently means that one's fate or social position may be involved. The need to defend oneself or one's interests becomes more obvious.

When the discussion turns to an analysis of friends or of beloved organizations, the fearful defenses become much more obvious. Then if the discussion turns to commentary upon some individual in the meeting, the person in question is likely to regard the comment as a personal attack. We have found that students are quite free to write reports analyzing the behavior of citizens in meetings and will discuss strong and weak points with a fine show of scientific spirit. But when called upon to deal as objectively with events on the campus involving friends and themselves, they will often flare up in emotional displays or refuse to comment lest their judgments be regarded as disloyalty.

Yet it is the ability to assess facts as they are in matters that are deeply important which modern man needs if he is to act intelligently in a complicated world.

It is probable that the fear of objectivity is, at base, an expression of insecurity. Men fear to look at their organizations, their lives, themselves because an unbiased view might expose some weakness they prefer to have hidden. An objective examination of some loved object is unwelcome because the defensive person fears exposure of something about which he already has conscious or unconscious doubts. Such people will not develop objectivity from exhortation. They may make progress toward this goal by being reassured that no one intends an attack, by gaining self-confidence in discussion and action, by becoming more mature persons to live in modern times.

The Tyranny of Reason

A student, commenting on a community committee meeting he had attended, said, "You pointed out that they [the citizens] could choose to do whatever they wanted to do. But the facts forced them to make the choice you approved of. So they did not feel free." He felt that the citizens had lost some of their freedom of choice by being forced to a certain decision by their own rational appraisal of the facts. Needless to say, the student was speaking for himself as well as for the representatives of the community in the meeting. He (and they perhaps) feared the tyranny of reason.

Many men, particularly in troubled times, fear intelligence, even their own intelligence. They prefer to cling to traditional fixed opinions, even though these be clearly irrational. There is greater security, greater seeming safety in the haven of a familiar opinion even though that harbor no longer be adequate. To trust to reason is to put out into an uncharted sea with no fixed landmarks of unshifting certainty. Like the early navigators who first ventured out of sight of land, the man who depends upon his reason must develop faith in himself and in his ability to read the navigational instruments of rationality.

The fear of the tyranny of reason may take a peculiar form in the discussion meeting which is attempting to develop objectivity. The fearful participant, if he does not protest vociferously, may spend a great amount of silent time in resisting the pull of the obvious, resisting the pull of his own intelligence. He may take out his discomfort in growling inwardly or *sotto voce* to his neighbor. Or after the meeting he may complain against others in the group with whom he disagrees or against the discussion leader who adds to his discomfort.

To deal with such fears blocking the road to objectivity is not easy. Progress toward the desired end is not likely to occur as long as the resisting individual is insecure. Fundamentally he fears to examine himself, his ideas, his associations, his friends, lest these prove less than satisfactory. A first step to achieving objectivity is the building of enough security and self-trust to overcome defensive fear.

The social scientist must labor constantly to cultivate a functioning objectivity in himself. In democratizing research, he seeks development of objectivity in the entire group that comes to investigate itself and to direct its own conscious growth.

Collective objectivity should be easier of achievement than the individual variety. It is easier to admit group sin than individual wrongdoing. It is easier to say "We have done wrong" than "I have done wrong." Confession of collective guilt leaves the individual some shred of personal alibi. It is the sense of collective responsibility that needs cultivation in the complicated modern world. This has its small beginning in projects of community collaboration which develop skill in democratic research.

There is more to collective objectivity than confession of group sin. The confession is a necessary part, but let it be free of the breast-beating self-condemnation which often characterizes individual admission of guilt. The end sought is not merely a blowing off of guilty emotion but a calm assumption of responsibility for past and future conduct. This is based upon an ability to make discriminating judgments about one's own group, to point to achievements and shortcomings without either undue pride or abject apology.

Progress toward the achievement of collective objectivity often goes through certain definite and observable stages.

1. *Disorganized Immaturity*

Unfortunately, disorganized immaturity is characteristic of many a community. There is lack of focused interest in public affairs, or those who might lead are separated into self-canceling factions. Achievement for the general good is thought of as a triumph for one small group as against the efforts of competitors. There is inability to think together. Frustrated inactivity is the result of activity limited to narrow groups whose appeal for support is largely emotional. The rationality that comes from a broad cooperative attack upon problems, the sense of responsible competence to handle one's fate—these are missing.

2. *Discovery of Challenging Need*

The fact that a community needs something is not sufficient evidence that the second stage has been reached. There must be awareness of a need strong enough to stir a few promising people from former inactivity, to bring together a significant number of formerly competing groups. The recognized and challenging need is the occasion for the formation of an over-all community coordinating council. This is the group which can attempt to achieve a collective objectivity as part of a program of action-research. The second stage is begun with some appreciative discovery of a challenging need. It is consummated with the coming together of people and factions to work in answer to the need.

3. *The Willingness to Learn*

The development of a community-wide group adequate to meet a challenging need is not the achievement of first effort. It comes as a result of growth which flows from a willingness to learn. Adults learn consciously only when they reach the maturity which allows them to admit some deficiency, some ignorance. A willingness to learn is a willingness to be changed. All this is most painful if such self-humbling is done before instructors possessing superior wisdom. It comes much more easily when all people in the situation confess to similar deficiencies and each is a participant in guiding the growth process. The scientific attitude calls for humbleness in the face of need, admission of inadequacy. The arrogance exhibited by some social scientists is not evidence of objectivity. The scientific state of mind is achieved only as a by-product of a willingness to learn.

4. *Self-Investigation*

The chairman of a county planning commission once came to us for help. Said he, "We know there is much wrong with our county, but we are not sure just what. Will you come in, make a survey, and tell us what is wrong?"

We refused.

"Well, aren't you supposed to make such studies? Isn't that part of your work?"

Said we, "No, we never carry on research *for* someone. We will be glad to work *with* you and help you draw conclusions about yourselves. But we will never tell you what we believe is wrong with you. That conclusion you will have to make for yourselves on the basis of information which we help you to gather."

Investigation of community need for practical use is preferably self-investigation. Experts, or those who disclaim expertness, like ourselves, can join forces with local leaders to bring whatever skill they possess under the discipline of responsible leaders who must press for action. Too often professional surveys, by their very excellence, have proved deterrents to action. It is easy to deny the conclusions of outsiders, whatever their competence, or to insist that their recommendations are impractical. If the road to hell is paved with good intentions, then the road to community frustration is often paved with good surveys.

Only when a significant body of citizens have come to accept some responsibility for the general welfare and have indicated a willingness to learn from the facts is a community self-survey in order. There are experts enough to help with such an endeavor, though many need watching lest they forget to subordinate their decisions to the needs of community self-direction. Literature is available also for guidance of those who would direct the process themselves.

But there is far more to research than the mere collecting of useful facts. There is involved also a procedure for solving immediate problems and thereby building a body of knowledge which will guide careful guessing and formulation of theory by "pure" social scientists. The ordinary citizen can become a contributor to the structure of tested knowledge about human beings which may one day be as imposing as the achievements of the physical scientists. The more immediate concern to the ordinary man, however, is that research processes give him an ability to solve his problems with an objectivity which grants him a new control over his own collective fate.

The self-guided research process continues through discussion, arrival at a decision by consensus, collective action to carry out the decision, keeping records of the entire procedure, and evaluation of results. The evaluation is carried on by the group's making use of records kept by its members. The method is one of self-study and self-criticism with suggestions from those social scientists who can humble themselves enough to allow their recommendations to stand on their own merit, under the testing of democratic experience.

5. *Continued Self-Analysis*

The process of self-analysis in the midst of many succeeding projects can go on indefinitely. Both the projects and the analysis must be meaningful to the people involved, in terms of their needs and their growing maturity. Many activities and many an evaluation will seem inadequate to the sophisticated scientist. But he will find fresh sources of data for his theorizing and a new source of insight into his fellow man if he will encourage and study democratic community self-research.

DEMOCRATIC DISCIPLINE

The shouting advocates of democracy have long overstressed the freedoms which citizens should enjoy as a birthright and understressed their obligations. They have often neglected to point out that democracy, to succeed, calls for disciplines as exacting as those imposed by any monarch or dictator. The difference is that democratic discipline must be self-imposed.

The pioneer experiences encouraged Americans to glory in independent difference, to wallow in freedom. The way in which America has given birth and continues to give birth to rival religious sects is one evidence of overstressed freedom, little disciplined by sense of social responsibility. The contemporary movement to bring various churches together in national association represents a tendency toward the responsibility of maturity.

The frontier has been closed for almost two generations, though the pioneer virtues are still trumpeted to the skies by nostalgic writers, movie directors, and orators. The time has arrived for development of personality skills and attitudes more consistent with the demands of an interdependent age. Some of the newer virtues which responsibility imposes are already discernible to a sensitive eye. A few can be listed as long as these do not prejudice our expectancy for others to appear with changing times.

A whole group of skills cluster about the need for men to work together rather than against each other. It was a great achievement when men learned that they could differ sharply and still respect each other. It is an even greater achievement when they learn to cooperate without eliminating their differences. Freedom to oppose each other is easier to achieve than discipline to unite.

The arrogance which assumed a know-it-all attitude was more useful in a simpler pioneer age. The humbleness which admits ignorance and the need to learn throughout life is necessary in a complicated era of rapid change. Traditional ideas confined learning to younger years set aside for schooling. The unashamed willingness to grow abandons such a limited definition and makes learning synonymous with living.

Discipline for What?

There are those who insist that some discipline imposed upon people is good for them. This applies, they believe, especially to the young. But self-discipline cannot be developed for discipline's sake only. It must have a justification in terms of challenging purposes. A democracy which overstresses freedom encourages the individual to believe that there is virtue in expressing one's opinion, fully and frequently. A democracy which stresses social obligation encourages the individual to hold his tongue and to speak only for the purpose of furthering important objectives. The objective for contemporary democracy should be less unrestrained freedom of expression for myself and more the encouragement of responsibility in my fellow citizens and in my group. Self-discipline is acceptable to me only when I see something beyond myself, something bigger and more significant than myself alone.

In the earlier days of democracy, skill in debate and denunciation have been held in high esteem. As democracy matures, skill in understanding becomes much more important. It is so easy to oppose and so satisfying in a childish way. It is so difficult to understand but so rewarding in growth toward responsibility.

The ability to understand another's point of view and struggles is necessary to scientific guessing. It can be cultivated. The first step is to watch one's own tongue. The next is to watch the other fellow. Attention given to his words, his facial expressions, his gestures, the way his hands move, will give clues concerning his inner peace or turmoil. It will increase sympathy for another man's struggle to express himself and to grow in conscious self-direction.

But the understanding required for democratic citizenship in the modern world of confusion and strife goes much farther. It calls for an appreciative knowledge of basic reasons for differences among men. The man who differs with me is not necessarily dishonest, or evil, or subversive, or deliberately wrongheaded. He may even accept the same facts which I accept. But he sees them in a different frame of reference, according to another interpretation. If I am to understand him I must, to some extent, school myself to see facts through his eyes, according to his background. I must go through the exercise of seeing facts drop into a new pattern, support a point of view other than my own, if I am to understand the thinking and loyalties of people on the other side of a conflict. After I come to a sympathetic realization of another man's honestly held frame of reference I can more easily avoid speaking to relieve my own frustrations and speak rather to help him grow. I can more readily contribute to the ongoing progress of the group of which both of us are members.

The discipline of mature democracy calls for citizens to surrender the joy of attacking an opponent in favor of an understanding which gives him the benefit of most doubts. The opposition is assumed to be as sincere and decent as are the people on "our" side.

The cultivation of understanding does not imply any weakening of conviction. In fact, it is the person who is unsure of his own beliefs who must constantly convince himself by ranting in attack upon some opposition. Those who are calmly sure of a position they have thought out are more likely to possess the objectivity which seeks understanding.

Understanding in Action

Understanding is more than a mere intellectual process, expressed verbally. If genuine, it results in action. There are those who insist that they sympathize with their opponents and tolerate them, but prefer to avoid association with them. This attitude shows, at best, incomplete understanding. The genuine article tends to create a desire to associate with people across the normally drawn lines of opposition.

When people give sympathetic recognition to the varying backgrounds and frames of reference that produce differences among men, they tend to discover the great truth that human beings have more common denominators which should unite them than disputes which separate them. All men hunger, seek security, need rest when they tire, are subject to disease, love their children, hope for a better future, need the reassurance of association with their fellows. These are some of the common needs and experiences which pull mature men and women together. Understanding produces the desire to make friends. The leading citizens of adequate democracy will seek to associate with opponents to discover basic common aspirations which reduce differences to their proper place of superficiality. This is a practical application of the religious teaching, "Love your enemy." It has the belated endorsement of psychiatry and psychology as the only basis for an understanding vital enough to overcome war-producing conflict.

To suggest that good citizens of the future should seek out and make common cause with their "enemies" may seem like extreme medicine. Perhaps it would be too much to expect that such a skill could become widespread in any population within a predictable time period. But it can be held up as an ideal to be approximated by a few community leaders, then by a few more and a few more as understanding cooperation gradually replaces denunciatory competition.

Patience Plus Persistence

A final discipline which democratic citizens must learn is patience coupled with determination to keep working. Permanent change in men is slow and unspectacular. The exciting events which make the newspaper headlines are usually superficial or, if significant, are but single episodes in a longer-drawn-out and quieter process. Impatient youth, revolutionaries, and would-be martyrs often talk as though they have to bring in some utopia by a single world-shaking and dramatic event. But those who seek permanent changes by democratic means will cultivate the patience to wait for men to grow into the maturity which is potentially theirs.

The genuine believer in democracy will realize also that utopia is always in the future. True democracy is so ideal that it will not ever be completely realized. It is always in process of becoming. Yet decisions must be made; matters cannot be discussed forever and action postponed until every last man has convinced himself. The hope for arrival at a general consensus should not be used as an alibi for inaction. Until men develop greater skill than they now possess in creative discussion, they must accept the probability that most decisions for action will represent a none-too-satisfactory compromise. Or decisions will be made by committees, legislative bodies, and elected officials in which the ordinary citizen feels he has had little voice. These he must accept with whatever good-humored long-suffering he can muster, while he presses for better decisions and for more creatively democratic processes of reaching decisions.

The virtue of patience can become a vice if it results in the folded hands of cheerful discouragement. It needs to be balanced by determined persistence to make improvement. The achievement of a proper balance between long-suffering and the resolution to right an obvious wrong is a delicate matter no man can teach. It must be learned by experience.

Teaching Mature Democracy

It would be so simple if orthodox ideas of education could be applied to the training of citizens for the democracy of a compli-cated age of interdependence. Merely have the proper authorities decide upon the skills needed, put these into a course or courses, and teach them to learners old and young. Even if authorities could agree upon any listing of virtues such as has been presented here (a most unlikely event) these could not be taught as lessons. They must be discovered by men and women in their own vital experi-ences and become incorporated into their personalities quietly and in answer to their needs.

We are far from having achieved any process for teaching mature democracy. But we have made a few tentative gestures which open up possibilities. Students joining with citizens in a community self-survey can prove excellent learning teachers of objectivity. They are good in this role because they are so obviously learners, because they lack the assurance of the trained person and the didactic man-ner of the teacher. They can share with citizens in collecting of information, in recording, in wondering about the interpretation and usefulness of the data.

Whenever we have a job of collecting data for a community self-appraisal we attempt to insist upon having citizens and students work side by side. We are not always as successful in obtaining citizen participation as we would desire. But we keep trying in the hope that we may be instrumental in cultivating more research objectivity.

One unexpected aid has come out of our experience. The Program of Community Dynamics publishes an annual report recording progress or its lack. This is addressed to fellow educators, community leaders, and supporters of the College. But it is sent also to citizen collaborators in ongoing projects; we do not wish to hide anything. Some of these collaborators have read these reports with intelligent discrimination. They then have discussed the general theory of community development with us, laying stress upon their understanding of the need for local self-direction. The publication which was planned as a report of progress for the Program has turned out to be a stimulant for objective self-analysis and an inspiration for the achievement of greater democratic maturity in some instances.

These are but feeble beginnings in the matter of democratizing research. We hope they indicate possible directions for more ambitious achievement.

A process of democratized research seems best calculated to teach some such virtues as have been described, in a fashion which is, in part, self-teaching. In action-research, carried on at a level of complication suitable to the understanding of participants, there is chance for the discovery of those habit skills which point toward mature democracy. The means for gaining information become also a means for achieving self-discipline.

A CHALLENGE TO SOCIAL SCIENTISTS

Research is a skill so far preempted by the scientific elite. As long as it is held exclusively by them, the method remains arrogant and the people researched tend to remain at an immature level of development. The problem for the social scientist is less to refine methods and more to make the point of view and tricks of the trade available to ordinary men and women as an essential contribution to maturity.

Spontaneous action by emerging community leaders will not inevitably become action-research. The self-disciplinary learning process does not necessarily occur automatically. It can be encouraged and expedited by those with some claim to scientific respectability. There is no more exciting and significant challenge to the contemporary social scientist than to democratize his skills and approach in order to make the research process available to ordinary men.

CHAPTER XI

Individual and Group

MAN is a creature of inconsistency and paradox. An observer would be foolhardy indeed to attempt to enumerate all the inconsistencies which make his species fascinating. But a few are pertinent for mention.

Men rise to a human level by developing personalities. Personalities are always nurtured by some group or civilization. Yet an over-strong, inflexible group can crush the personalities it helped create. The twentieth century has seen multitudes of men seek importance by identifying themselves with an all-powerful state which has rewarded their faithfulness by destroying them as independent personalities.

Men as personalities have developed an unshakable conviction that they possess a free will, have freedom to make choices. Yet down through the ages the vast majority of men have lived the life of slaves, serfs, or pawns in a game played by others. The conviction of freedom persists in modern times in spite of widespread feelings of helplessness. Many modern men feel that they are victims of decisions beyond their control, that they are continually being dragged into wars which they do not want. When the feeling of helplessness becomes most overwhelming, some men exercise their freedom by choosing to inflict upon themselves a high degree of regimented group control.

Those with sturdier belief in freedom tend to make a virtue of revolt. It is they who have kept alive the tradition that it is clever and heroic to challenge constituted authority of whatever nature or for whatever cause. Some of the most admirable figures of democracy's younger years have been those who called for liberty or death in the face of some tyranny which deserved defiance. Yet in the modern interdependent world, revolt indulged in for revolt's sake will almost inevitably bring on the tyranny which the free man abhors.

Is freedom doomed, then, betrayed by both its fair-weather friends and its ill-advised supporters? Not necessarily. Some balance between the claims of individual freedom and the needs for living together in a complicated world must be achieved if life is to be tolerable for free men.

The inconsistencies of men may be sardonically amusing. They offer no guide for conduct in a difficult period of growth. Only shared and applied intelligence can serve that function.

DOES IT MAKE SENSE?

Life must make sense. This is the one demand that all men make of the universe. This is the demand which proves that human beings are human. So essential to men is an explanation of life that many have been willing to accept a clearly nonsensical meaning in preference to chaotic meaninglessness. A stubborn clinging to a particular belief through torture and martyrdom testifies less to the correctness of the particular credo than to man's need to have some belief. And the belief is a product of a meaningful group.

Understanding Diversity

Such philosophic conclusions are tested by students in community dynamics as a result of their contact with citizens. We have found that assumptions about a dull uniformity of personalities in rural America are mistaken. There is wide variety based upon affiliation with widely differing organizations, which make sense to each individual.

In one crossroads settlement boasting a population of approximately four hundred there were three churches. When a newly formed community council proposed to develop a recreation program for young people, there was wide difference in attitude on the part of the three ministers. One supported the proposal wholeheartedly. A second informed students that he was for recreation activities. He would "allow" his parishioners to cooperate, but he could give no time himself, since he must devote full time to religion. "Isn't this a type of religion in action?" asked the students of each other in discussion.

The third minister would have nothing to do with "worldly" activities such as recreation. Why? Because he looked for the coming of the millennium shortly, as soon as the plight of the human race was beyond all hope. Anyone who sought to improve conditions in this imperfect world was delaying the day of the coming of the Messiah in all his glory. Therefore he was actively opposed and advised his followers to concentrate attention upon their own salvation.

The recreation program was organized and carried on with student help. But in order to make it serve its purpose, some understanding of differences in belief and response to an activity which seemed utterly legitimate was necessary. Student impatience with seeming obtuseness was ultimately replaced with an interpretive understanding that led to sympathy. This change came about as a result of examining the group affiliations of each man, the associations that provided each with emotional sustenance. The only way to avoid the arrogance of a callow objectivity that examines other people with superiority was to admit that all men are shaped by the affiliations which make sense to them. Students and professors in the discussion were no exception. Their peculiar beliefs were subject to the same scrutiny.

When a deliberate attempt is made to develop unity without destroying diversity, differences based upon group loyalty become a matter of daily discourse. One community council had as a basic purpose the bringing together of Protestants, Jews, and Catholics, Negroes and whites. One of the active committees seeking to promote better employment opportunities irrespective of race, sex, or place of origin was composed of a Methodist minister, a Lutheran pastor, and a Catholic priest. Other councils have sought better relations between labor and management, farmers and city folk, older residents and poor "scapegoat" newcomers. In no case is an attempt made to erase or overlook differences. Rather each group loyalty is studied for its possible contribution to unity. Each group is encouraged to take pride in its own uniqueness, as a step on the way to community integration.

Every man must belong somewhere. In order to have status with his universe, with his fellows, with himself, he must have a place of recognition. The local small community is the place in which he can find meaning for himself without risking the loss of freedom which the gaining of meaning in the mass way entails.

Making Freedom Possible

To desperate people meaning is more important than freedom. In the agonies which followed the First World War and the great depression, men by the million accepted slaveries which made sense rather than suffer an uncontrolled chaos which was unintelligible. Has something the same happened after the Second World War and during the frightened uncertainties of East-West conflict? The notion has been advanced that the freedom granted by democracy comes only to those who possess some economic ease. Is it available also only to those who are not harassed by the fear that life may have lost meaning?

As long as men remain primarily the victims rather than the directors of their group associations, they cannot enjoy any major freedom. Freedom comes not in individual revolt against the tyranny of any group. It comes rather in the intelligent choice and reshaping of groups which shall grant the kind of meaning to life which fulfills the individual. If men gain significance from the groups that give them status, they can learn to control those same groups through exercise of group intelligence.

This fact constitutes the major opportunity for community educators. To increase men's collective control over the groups that control men—that is to increase freedom. The modern free man becomes slave neither to tradition nor to the newer tyrannies which offer themselves as answer to man's desperate need to belong. The free man can remain free only as he gains intelligent collective control over the groups which are significant to him. The community educator will recognize that the process of gaining collective control is a gradual one, beginning at the simple community level.

An Era of Diminishing Meaning

The modern age has been devastating to the egos of ordinary men. Their meaning and importance have been diminishing often to the point of desperation, even in the countries which still maintain a considerable amount of freedom.

The individual citizen loses significance, even in his own eyes. The feeling grows that great affairs are too complicated or on too grand a scale for him to have a decision in them. Important questions are seldom referred to his opinion in elections. Indeed, it would be next to impossible to have an electoral referendum on each issue which touches the lives of citizens for good or for ill. Decisions are therefore made without reference to those they affect, or matters are allowed to drift without policy or direction.

Real controls, therefore, seem to be in the hands of others. Among the villains blamed for a general sense of helplessness are:

Politicians. "All you can do is throw out those in power and put in some others equally bad."

Owners or controllers of newspapers, radios, industries, labor unions, and other accumulations of power. The feeling against these people much exaggerates their strength and freedom of decision.

Leaders of enemy nations, totalitarian dictators and their henchmen. The fear and condemnation here are likely to be hysterical, partly because devils never seen are more frightening than those who occasionally appear in the flesh, partly because the dictators seem beyond the reach of human and humane influence.

An inexorable and unfriendly fate. So strong is men's belief in their own free will, however, that only a few deeply sunk in hopeless helplessness will accept a doctrine of fatal inevitability.

Whatever the villains, a sense of individual impotence grows. When the individual diminishes in importance and in self-directed responsibility he is driven to make begging or pressuring appeal to distant and probably unsympathetic authority to gain his ends.

The individual citizen feels divorced from authority. His government is no longer the collectivity of all of us working together; it is a separate entity to be feared, condemned, and placated. The same divorce between citizen-member-contributor and authority is to be observed in the case of nongovernmental organizations which carry important public functions, such as churches, Y.M.C.A.'s, community chests, private hospitals, and schools. These we all regard as separate entities apart from "ourselves" with a life of their own, over which "we" can have little control, even though they were set up to serve "us."

Because the conviction grows that the real responsibility of decision lies with distant, self-determining authority, there is little impulse toward broad-scale citizen organization. Why seek to develop groups, meaningful because able to guide the future, when these are foredoomed to impotence? There is no need to cultivate the self-discipline of responsible democratic action across the lines of conflict. It is enough to seek only association with a few like-minded people in order to indulge in the irresponsibility of lobbying with, or putting pressure upon, resisting officials.

An era which calls for citizens who can think and act in terms of the welfare of everyone has seen citizens go into groups which represent social fragments. Lack of identity with any geographic community and the rootlessness which is characteristic of transients and suburbanites tend to destroy local sense of belonging. The general welfare of the community seems unimportant because the community is unimportant. Instead the labor union, chamber of commerce, service club, racial or religious organization with national or international ties becomes the meaningful group. These are all fragmentary because interested primarily in promoting the welfare of a membership which is always but one part of a population.

The member of a special interest pressure group is a fragmentary man. The citizen of a community is potentially a whole man. The dignity of the individual can be rediscovered by membership in a group that plans for general welfare. The lack of such a group makes for the despair of impotence. And despair is the open invitation to dictatorship.

So great is man's need to belong significantly that a continued denial of a legitimate answer leads in time to a caricature of an answer. The answer in terms of democratic legitimacy and in terms of individual dignity is to find sense of community in the intimacy of some local face-to-face group. The alternative is to turn in frustrated desperation to the caricature found in belonging to a national group of regimentation offered by some dictator on the way to power.

RESCUING COMMUNITIES?

At this point the community educator leaps forward, with stars in his eyes. Here is his chance to rescue the community and the human race simultaneously. Man can find the dignity of his own personality only in the warmth of human association. He can gain his freedom only by becoming a responsible member of a self-directing group. The more inclusive the group, the greater the freedom. Let us then recapture the vitality of communities as the groups which will make men responsible and free.

The stars in the eyes fade with experience. The gloomy fact is that most men exhibit a remarkable indifference to all-inclusive organization—which includes disliked members of a community. And communities occasionally resist being revitalized. The high death rate among community councils is common knowledge to impatient organizers. Men seem to prefer membership in the separating organizations which break social living into fragments, and which, as a consequence, wield a much smaller conscious control over their own fate.

The Vitality of the Fragments

Every organizer of community life is familiar with this fact: that citizens normally exhibit greater loyalty to organizations representing minority interest than to those devoted to the welfare of all. Even when community councils are successful, they often grow in an atmosphere of apparent rivalry with less-inclusive organizations. Representatives to the council require continual encouragement to attend meetings, remarking that the council is just "one more organization making a demand on our time." Why should fragmentary associations command more loyalty than the more universal significance and greater collective power of an organization devoted to the welfare of the whole community?

The teachings of a society which takes pride in competition encourage men to prefer conflicting fragments rather than cooperative responsibility. In such an atmosphere it is usually assumed without question that one organization or group can prosper only at the expense of some other interest. Latent good will in individuals remains latent. And men learn to take satisfaction in the minor achievements of smaller, less significant associations. The big accomplishments which grow out of a wholistic view of community life take time. Men would rather put faith in the lesser goal than in the great hope of mutual dependence. The first calls for comfortably conventional action. The second calls for effort beyond tradition and a risking of the future in the hands of former rivals. The need for "belonging" leads men to cling to that which exists rather than risk a greater prize from something which possibly may not succeed.

Because of the need to survive and prosper in the midst of competition, fragmentary organizations become institutions. Instead of depending upon the voluntary action that arises from spontaneous good will, institutions tend to achieve attendance and loyalty through pressure. An institution develops a set structure of ranks and officers and a creed with supporting rituals; it usually employs organizers to hold the whole complication together. Many are the devices used to hold loyalty against all rivals. Among churches these range all the way from badges for faithful attendance, to social pressure, to threat of heavenly reprisal. Among labor unions, enforced membership is often guaranteed by checkoff or ostracism occasionally supplemented by violence. Among business organizations, loyalty is sought by social pressures applied through friendship or at times by such devices as refusal of, or calling of, loans.

Pitted against this array of energetic coercions, the community as a group has to offer only a gentle pull of wholeness and cooperative good will. Even when a community council employs an executive secretary, he should not apply the same kind of pressures used by the fragmentary constituent organizations; his job is to persuade these parts to become integrated without losing their identity. Despite the inequality of pull upon men's loyalties, experience leads us to believe that the community can become the central group for most men, if organizers are patient and skillful enough. Human beings do not jump from the fragments of a competitive age to the wholeness of democratic cooperation in a single leap. The art of voluntary good will may at first seem hopeless and unrewarded in an age of pressure. But it carries within itself its own reward, an increased collective control over the future.

The promoter who seeks to reestablish a sense of community in the lives of people must avoid a constant temptation—to gain results by becoming himself a rival applier of pressure. Much of the sense of helplessness to be found in modern man grows out of the conviction that he can do so little merely because he wants to. He lives in a civilization which coerces and exhorts him at every turn. The institution he loves dares not trust his spontaneous loyalty. His educational progress was governed by threats of poor marks or failure. Advertising flaunted everywhere calls upon him to eat the proper foods, wear the right clothes, smoke the pressured brand of tobacco. Even his generous impulses must be regimented. He is seldom allowed to give of his substance for the need of others when he feels the impulse. He must make a contribution during a "drive." In an age of organization even the desire to do good must be held in check until the exhortation comes from the assigned solicitor.

It is easy to conclude that there is no place for him who would wait for decency and generosity to prevail as a result of maturation. But for the community to become the group which gives a meaning of wholeness to men's lives, it must be accepted spontaneously as an answer to men's need. The super-persuasion of a high-pressure civilization is the enemy of meaning, which must be discovered in the quiet experience of belonging to a group that yields a comprehensible wholeness.

The conscientious community educator will use all the means of publicity at his disposal. But his purpose remains that of supplying the information necessary for citizens to make up their own minds. Community loyalty which must be regimented is unstable and must be periodically reregimented. Whatever publicity or promotion is used therefore must be carefully chosen to increase self-chosen initiative.

Community—A New Experience

The community educator who succeeds in promoting a constant buzz of activity on the part of councils and committees may well be a failure at his larger task. If he relies only upon the pressure methods of commercial promotion, he dooms his efforts to the second-best rating of imitation. But even worse, he has failed to introduce men to a new kind of experience desperately needed in an age of overpersuasion. Men need an area of their lives in which they can do the good thing because they want to, can be free from the harassment of things that must be done under pressure. The achievement of a sense of community, spontaneously sought and co-operatively planned, introduces a contrasting type of experience to lives truncated by diminishing responsibility and limited meaning.

The community often fails as a group giving the meaning of wholeness to men, because it is operated merely as another rival fragment. It fails too because the experience of wholeness is new to most modern men. The fragments, with their narrower objectives and pressure tactics, are more real. Only gradually can experience with an all-inclusive group broaden the area of self-chosen autonomy.

Those who would press for meaning in modern life may as well recognize that the fragmentation of life will be with us for a long time. The reduction in time required to travel around the world has resulted not in a drawing together of peoples but in increased nervous fear of difference. The necessity for breaking down barriers of religion, class, or race, made obvious in a complicated age, has often resulted in a closing of ranks by minorities against one another. The organizer of a community council frequently is discouraged to discover that representatives from fragmentary groupings have come together, not to learn cooperation but to find a forum for pleading their particular narrow causes. The labor union representative will come for the express purpose of condemning his "oppressors." The spokesman for Negroes will seize the opportunity to give voice to the grievances of his subgroup. The representative of wealth and comfort will give a firm endorsement of things as they are in the best of all possible worlds. Each is thinking primarily of the aims and welfare of his own particular fragment. The ability and willingness to think in terms of the welfare of all will grow. But the process of growth is slow and we are only beginning to learn how to hasten it.

The times cry out for men who can rise above the grievances and defensive reactions of their own social fragments. Even when those grievances are legitimate, as in the case of an underprivileged minority like the Negroes in the United States, most progress toward achieving their own ends is made when the disadvantaged people can look beyond their immediate frustrations and work with others for general community betterment. Much patience is required to wait until men's thinking can rise from the painful particular grievance to the creativity of general welfare.

The Test of Ultimate Vitality

A community which includes all, which is devoted to the welfare of all in ever-widening circles, which becomes the prototype for world-wide cooperation is the best group unit available to give men responsible significance. But it does not spring into life at the call of hopeful community organizers. It is built slowly, by introducing a new type of experience in contrast to much of the life of the modern age.

What are the essential elements that will lead to growth of community vitality? The kind of community is not as important as the relationships that grow within it. There is no magic in the small town or in rural life, despite the sometimes emotional appeal for a return to the simplicity of yesteryear. There is virtue in smallness of the operating unit. The group which meets again and again to plan, work, and evaluate should allow for an intimacy of give-and-take. The universe begins to take on meaning when it responds. The response comes best in a face-to-face situation.

Sense of community does not develop out of mere geographic living together. Such physical nearness needs to be supplemented by a warm sense of companionship which flows from much meeting together and sharing of purposes—all this without eliminating diversity. As long as there is more warmth of human association in fragmentary groups than in the assemblage of the whole, the latter will have but a feeble vitality.

A community association, to survive, must shortly address itself to problems of real concern to citizens. It must demonstrate that it possesses greater power over the future than do the fragmentary constituents. To the warmth of human association is then added a new maturity of self-determining responsibility. The individual citizen is significant because his association is significant.

The success sought is not that which comes from applying pressure by lobbying. The begging appeal for favors or the coercing by threat or promise directed against legislator or administrator does little to increase the dignity of the citizen. This is gained rather in the experience of discovering a job to be done, then making a plan and carrying it through to completion. This experience, even with some minor achievement at first, gives a new dignity and significance to citizen-participants.

Any community association which meets these essential tests is on the road to expanding vitality. The tests are not those of success in accomplishment, merely. They are based more on the quality of personal experience of those who are active in a community. The final evaluation is not one which can be made on paper by an outsider. It must be found in the experience and lives of the participants. The ultimate test of vitality for any community lies in whether or not its citizens develop a meaningful sense of belonging, which increases their stature.

A Never-Ending Search

For a long time to come, modern man will continue his search for a group significant enough to give him significance. A happy announcement that the community is *the* group solves no problem. The question of *which* community remains, in an age when men tend to be separated from geographic loyalty. The details of democratic functioning for personal and social growth will require endless experimentation. This in spite of all guiding generalizations put down by this or any other writer.

The failure of a community effort calls not for discouragement but for fresh effort. Even more, a success indicates not an end but need for continued experiment. There is a basic need of human aspiration to be met. Neither failure nor success should interfere with the search. A group is to be developed and revised according to changing need, a group that satisfies man's need to belong. A sense of community is to be found which frees personalities by encouraging voluntary choice of responsibility, which maintains a balance between group discipline and self-discipline.

Failure Should Be No Deterrent

Community promotion efforts fail much more often than hopeful promoters would desire. The word "failure" is used for at least two kinds of events: the community organization which never seems to live up to its promise and the council that never is formed or disintegrates. The first should never be regarded as a failure. For human accomplishment will always fall short of aspiration—or the aspiration was unworthy. But when people who are to be benefited refuse to respond, stay away from meetings, come for a few times and then develop an apologetic indifference, or when they give up the struggle in the face of disappointment and retire once more into their fragmentary lives, then indeed has failure come.

Discouragement or a condemnation of such "stupid people who fail to cooperate with those who are trying to help them" is the easy response to failure. A more realistic and intelligent reaction is an analysis of possible causes, leading to a decision on next steps to be taken. Men's refusal to become active members of any particular group does not mean that they are lacking in need for significant belonging.

The disappointed community organizer may conclude, on analysis, that the defeat of his efforts can be blamed upon people's greater readiness to respond to fragmentary organizations in a competitive age. He should also, however, examine his own possible failures. Has there been a poor choice of social unit to be encouraged toward unity? In rural areas, should each little settlement attempt organization, or each township, or county, or is there some other choice of social unit more meaningful to people? In cities, is a block or a neighborhood or a housing development or city ward the social unit that will mean most to people? Then, which type of organization is best—an over-all planning council or a committee set up to work on some narrow problem, or some other approach? Probably a wide variety of solutions will be found depending upon differences in local situations and differences among people. This diversity means that there will inevitably be many failures of efforts before workable answers are found for hundreds of varied communities.

The frustrated organizer must also give critical examination to his own impatience. Men learn to lift their eyes from the immediate particular to the long-run over-all good only slowly. Too often representatives of fragmentary groups come together only to eye each other with suspicion. It may be a matter of months or years before a vital warmth of intimacy develops. The introduction either of planning on too grand a scale or of serious controversy before some loyalty to a group of the whole has grown often proves fatal.

Whatever the causes of setback, failure should act as a stimulus to thought and further experiment. Although no one enjoys having his hopes frustrated, we must admit ruefully that we have usually learned more from a failure than from a success.

Success Merely Points the Way

A community effort which succeeds does not indicate that the people have arrived; rather that they are on the way. Too often success is a sedative, not a stimulant.

Community accomplishment is likely to be measured by values irrelevant to maturation processes in citizens. Success is given a definition that grows out of competition between fragmentary groups: huge numbers of people attending a meeting, big headlines, large sums of money collected, a park laid out or building constructed. These are often important but are the obvious events that hide the subtle and more important achievements. The fact that people are active and enthusiastic in considerable number proves that some need is being met. Is this part of their growth toward cooperative responsibility? Are they coming to have a warm sense of belonging to a meaningful whole which grants them greater individual dignity? The superficial kind of success that can be photographed and written up in a news article can easily obscure these major objectives. A tendency to be too joyful about first achievements diminishes the determination to keep working for the long-run success.

When the community educator can continually remind himself that he is not a past master but a learner, he may himself avoid the dangers flowing from success. He proves himself an educator by raising questions which point toward continued learning on the part of citizens. To those possessing the flexibility to learn, an achievement that calls for congratulation is merely a signpost along the road. The goals are so important that any success can be, at best, only an approximation.

Creative Cooperation

All men cooperate with their fellows, some willingly, some under compulsion. Some work with others for selfish, fragmentary ends; others cooperate for mutual benefit in an expanding whole. There is little to be admired in the mere act of working together. Slaves do that. Creative cooperation must be voluntary and intelligently directed toward democratically chosen goals. In the modern world, intelligence calls for the democratically choosing group to be all-inclusive, at the basic community level and more and more in the complicated human associations beyond.

Men cling to the limited goals of fragmentary organizations out of something more than mere perversity or traditionalism. They fear (consciously or unconsciously) that their own organization, religion, race, class, or nation can gain and hold advantages only at the price of disadvantage to supposed rivals. They assume (consciously or unconsciously) that there is an insufficient quantity of the good things men want to go around. The good things include adequate food and clothing, a decent home, conveniences of modern life, and luxuries. They include also such insubstantial things as a job and advancement, the privilege of living in "better" sections of town, membership in "exclusive" churches and clubs, and sharing in other man-made scarcities.

The assumption of an inevitable scarcity of material goods has been true for most of the long, tragic history of mankind. The assumption is probably no longer true.* It is difficult to make a

* On food alone see Charles W. Kellogg, *Soils, Food and People,* UNESCO publication, and "Opportunities for World Abundance," *Journal of Politics,* vol. 13 (1951).

dogmatic, flat-footed statement about the ability of the human race to produce enough, if it made full use of the technical "know-how" already available, on large scale. Not only is the technical knowledge limited to a small number of nations, whose standards of living are high, but the "advanced" countries have been unwilling to unleash full productivity (except in time of war). Their reluctance to produce to the maximum is based more upon a fear that there will be an insufficient number of buyers with ability to buy than upon a fear of inability to produce more. There is untapped production potential in the technically advanced nations. There is obviously even more in the underdeveloped parts of the world.

Whether a humanity-wide era of material plenty waits upon the full exploitation of the earth's resources and the scientific productive ability of man could well be debated. One thing is clear: there would be much, much more available for distribution if men could overcome their fear of scarcity, share their "know-how," and encourage the self-motivated initiative of their fellows everywhere. It is fearful clinging to lesser fragmentary goals that hampers a cooperation which would point toward production of material goods beyond the dreams of those who are at present comfortable.

Actually, it is now technically possible to feed the entire American nation adequately, without curtailing anyone's diet. In time it would probably be possible to feed the entire human race, unless population increases outran production of food. In any American community, it would be technically and financially feasible to provide a decent home for every family, including even the usually disinherited minority, without reducing standards for those now well housed. As for those people whose hold upon personal security is so weak that they must constantly remind themselves of the artificial superiority of their social fragment, there is little place for them in an era of shared abundance. The attitude of exclusiveness contributes to scarcity. In the twentieth century the deterrents to abundance are less in technology and more in men's minds and institutions.

The era of abundant sharing can be begun on a small scale in the local community. It can be a by-product of community-wide belonging to an all-inclusive group. The proposer of community betterment frequently operates in an atmosphere of anticipated opposition. Whatever improvements are attempted, he assumes, will bring forth organized objection from those who feel their own privileges are threatened. Too often his fears are justified. If he could assure the opposition that real improvements can be found which will make life better for everyone, he would stand a better chance of gradually breaking down the attitudes of those who cling defensively to the present.

Any change, no matter how beneficent, will inconvenience someone. Even though there be long-run advantages clearly promised, the temporary disturbance of established habits is painful. The problem is to replace a fear that present advantages are under attack from jealous competitors with the idea that the future can be ever-expanding when all people work together, each with confidence in the good motives of the others.

There are ready-made oppositions for each proposed improvement. Better schools are typically opposed by taxpayers' associations, housing projects by real-estate and property owners' organizations. Improvement of race relations will often call forth attack from both employers and labor unions. The list is long and discouraging. It will vary according to each local situation. These oppositions are not dissolved by the assurance that everyone will be better off when nervous defense of fragmentary advantage is replaced by the courage for the future which grows out of creative cooperation. They dissolve only in the experience of meeting together, planning and working together in a fashion that takes the needs of all into consideration. They dissolve as erstwhile opponents come to have confidence in the good will of each other in the warmth of all-inclusive community association.

The task for the community educator may be never ending. But it is pregnant with challenging possibilities. To find significant meaning for individual lives is to discover freedom in a group that encourages creative cooperation, is to lay a local basis for an era of abundant sharing. The pattern for local sharing of responsibility and benefit can become the pattern for sharing on national and international scale.

A Tragic Paradox

One of the strangest and saddest of paradoxes is this: men ever tend to shut themselves away in mutually distrustful and mutually destructive groups, when it is clear that they would all benefit by getting together. The most admired of the ethical seers of the ages have understood and preached the advantages of cooperation. The religious organizations which call upon their names, each claiming the final universal meaning of life, have often been among the most divisive of groupings. Their divisiveness grows out of an insistence that cooperation can occur only on their own terms, by everyone's accepting their particular view of life. The paradox of separateness in the face of man's need for togetherness is not relieved by enforced conformity. It can be met only experimentally by having the separate fragments come together to find greater freedom in voluntary grouping that welcomes difference. The search for such groups begins at the face-to-face community level.

The search is worth the effort even as a perpetual job. No man limited by the narrow interests of his social fragment can predict the creative possibilities of self-realizing cooperation.

CHAPTER XII

A Practitioner's Handbook

EVERY time a community makes conspicuous growth, some one person will usually be found as prime initiator. Even those situations which seem poised on tiptoe ready for great achievement usually wait for the extra push that the proper personality can give. Such an individual is a practitioner of the art of community development.

The practitioner may be an outsider with humanitarian or research interest. He may be a citizen-at-home who develops a vision of unrealized possibilities. He may be a professional, imported by some organization devoted to public good. He should be both philosopher and practical man of affairs, with emphasis on the practical.

There are many kinds of practitioners operating in multitudes of communities. Their actual practices will depend upon their objectives and philosophy. Our handbook recommendations point toward a particular kind of community promoter. He is less the one who:

Puts on huge publicity campaigns.
Persuades people, in the mass, to support prechosen ideas.
Builds buildings or other great physical facilities.
Raises large sums of money.
Develops successful, permanent institutions.

He may become involved in all such matters from time to time. But he finds greater satisfaction in being the one who:

Searches for the kind of organization that matures and frees men.
Encourages growth of leadership ability.
Promotes the experience of community.

The practitioner we are recommending accepts a role of humbleness to seek his triumphs in the lives of others. He is a cultivator of the art of applied patience. His motto might well be "Suggest, Wait, and Act When the Group Is Ready!"

MISTAKES TO AVOID

In claiming status as amateurs, we sometimes insist that at least we have learned some things not to do. A few "don'ts" can be listed, if it be understood that we reserve the right to learn from the mistakes of the future. Neither the negative suggestions nor the positive ones that follow are complete.

Don't Know It All

There is nothing quite so oppressive as the man who always has the answer, who never makes a mistake. Make a few, or rather admit those you make. It may hurt at the time, but in the end the admission will strengthen you in the eyes of collaborators—provided there are a few good ideas to scatter among the mistakes.

Don't Become Impatient

People will change to accept responsibility only at their own pace. They cannot be pushed faster, though it is possible to direct their attention to need and to invite initiative. Do not give up if matters move slowly. Keep a gentle pressure on the situation. Then when people are ready to act, things will often move with breathtaking speed.

Don't Press

When some development seems proper to you, offer a suggestion, raise a question, but don't press. If no one finds the idea challenging, let it rest for a time. It can be repeated in a different form later. But it will never become a contribution to the growth of citizen collaborators unless they adopt it as their own.

Don't Argue

Differ with people, yes. State the points on which you differ as clearly and cheerfully as possible. Point out that all intelligent people have ideas of their own. Take pride in the differences, yours and theirs. But avoid a defense of your own position.

Don't Become Worried and Harassed

Because community work is time-consuming, puts pressure upon anyone who takes responsibility, may call for attention at any hour of the twenty-four and any day of the week, it can be wearisome. It is easy to accept more assignments than any one person can fulfill. Then the practitioner tends to become a nervous wreck, rushing from half-baked decision to half-completed task. The writer is a major authority on such matters. This unhappy state can be avoided by organization of time and the courage to say an occasional "No."

Don't Lose the Sense of Humor

It is easy to do so when overbusy and overworried. A cheerful manner will both ease those situations which might cause worry and make their solution easier. Realize, though, that for some people "Life is real, life is earnest." For them humor may seem flippant unless it is accompanied by a serious determination to meet the problem at hand.

Don't Interrupt

Let people finish when they are thinking and speaking, even though their efforts be halting. Try to understand; try to help them express themselves more clearly. Then, if possible, accept and build upon their ideas.

Don't Keep the Center of the Stage

Let the other fellow shine. Your success comes in the growth of the leader who develops as a result of your influence. Even when you could do it better or when your idea has been preempted, let the citizen collaborator take the spotlight. If it becomes necessary to be important for a short time, pass the glory on to someone else quickly.

Don't Be Too Elated When Praised

Anyone enjoys praise or flattery. And you may even deserve it. But keep in mind when the bouquets are being passed that the brickbats will come later. Try to avoid an upset of equilibrium from either extreme.

Don't Be Unhappy When Criticized

You will be criticized if you are accomplishing anything worth while. Accept the negative comment with an attentive ear. Realize that the unpleasant remarks may come as much from the emotional needs of the critic as from an appraisal of your own blundering. Accept the criticism as evidence that something may be wrong. Try to correct your own ineptitude, which may not be the point mentioned in the criticism at all. No man is perfect and there may be some suggestion for improvement even in an ill-mannered attack.

Don't Defend Yourself if Attacked

Let the attack come. Try to create a permissive atmosphere that will allow the whole story to come out. Be interested and concerned, not defensive or alarmed. Admit at least a few failings which the critic has pointed out and which are true. To find a few failings ascribable to any of us fallible mortals—that is easy. To admit these openly—that is much more difficult. If possible, work up the courage to apologize for some shortcomings. But the apology must be sincere, not merely an act for effect. Hope and expect that the attackers, if allowed to complete their story, will themselves eventually partially reverse their position, will begin to apologize. Then out of the misunderstanding may come a new positive relationship of mutual trust. Act in such a way as to help even your critics to achieve greater maturity. And, after all, they may prove to be right when you think things over.

Don't Be Noble

The suffering demeanor of the conscious martyr can be infuriating or the occasion for defensive laughter. The noble characters of history had the irritating habit of suffering for the right. That inevitably reduced the rest of the human race who opposed them to being wrong. No one enjoys that predicament and as a consequence there is always a barrier between the saint and ordinary mortals. You, as a community educator, must work with ordinary people. If you are a saint, let this fact be discovered after you are dead. During life sainthood can be a serious handicap.

Don't Become Alarmed When People Lose Maturity

Regression to childish behavior is common to all humanity, especially when some maturity is only newly acquired. The childishness will probably pass if not taken too seriously. Even community educators have their moments when maturity slips.

Don't Be Devious and Clever

Be as direct and forthright as possible. State your purposes casually and in terms of the motives the citizen collaborator will understand. Otherwise debate over differing philosophic fine points and over concern with methodology can easily stand in the way of decisions for action.

Don't Educate People by Instructing Them

Realize that the best education grows out of mutual sharing in which you learn along with your collaborator. People grow most rapidly toward maturity by their own choice, with their own consent. Learning comes best, not by instruction, but by real experience analyzed in discussion.

Don't Become a Partisan for Reform

There will be those people in any community whose grievance causes them to press for direct action of some sort. Even though the suggested reform be a legitimate one in the eyes of the community educator, his job is neither to support the proposed change nor to oppose it. He is a mediator devoted to bringing the contending factions together, concerned to help all find an even better solution to problems than any yet proposed. There is every place for proponents of change but this is not the role for the community educator. The roles of the reformer and of the mediator cannot be mixed in the same person at the same time.

Don't Wait for Disputes to Come to You

Though you be a mediator, do not sit in Buddha-like contemplation waiting for a call to come for your services. A good community educator is active; he is on the alert for opportunities which might contribute to the growth of citizens toward maturity. Many conflicts could be handled on a more constructive basis if they were brought to mediation before they reach the stage of screaming headlines. By the time sensationally reportable events have taken place, the opposing sides in a dispute have been lined up and the stubborn desire to save face will not allow creative compromise. The good community educator deliberately puts himself in the middle of difficult situations, hoping to draw attention to need for reform, even though he does not himself advocate any proposed solution.

Don't Lose the Ability to Marvel at the Way Things Work Out

We are sometimes convinced that success comes to community projects in spite of our best efforts as well as because of them. When the practitioner is so sure of human processes that he can predict results with blasé assurance, his utility is considerably diminished. And he has lost the joy of looking for the unexpected.

Don't Expect to Live Up Fully to All These "Don'ts"

No one is that good.

In any handbook there is always grave danger that a reader will accept the recommendations as if they were a bag of tricks, or a formula for success. In point of fact, the writer may seem to give support to such a view by using the term "tricks of the trade." Indeed, there are certain ways of doing things that can be advised with some assurance, since they have often produced desired results. But any faithfulness to these suggestions could easily prove disastrous. So the final "don't" is:

Don't Adopt Any Bag of Tricks

Any formulalike system of dealing with people must be flexible to allow adaptation to unpredictable situations. A bag of tricks will not substitute for intelligence. The important matter in this handbook is not the recommended methods for handling community problems but the spirit that lies back of them. All together they call for a philosophy of dealing with one's fellow man and for a kind of person who embodies that philosophy. If the point of view and spirit can be understood, the detailed suggestions drop into their proper minor place.

THE COMMUNITY ON THE WAY TO UNITY

A conglomeration of people living near each other is not necessarily a community. It gradually becomes one as the people achieve a sense of belonging to one another. The hopeful practitioner tries to add overtones of unity to geographic proximity.

What Is the Role of the Practitioner?

The role of the educator-promoter depends upon the manner of his arrival upon the scene. If he is a local resident, he is more readily accepted as a fellow learner but may find it necessary to overcome the handicap of identification with certain factions or organizations. If he is an outsider, he can more easily maintain an attitude of disinterested objectivity but must overcome the handicap of assumption that he is an expert who knows just what to do. He should determine in advance whether he wishes to be regarded as a member of the community or as an outside stimulator.

In both cases he should assume an attitude of nonaggressive friendliness. He should offer himself and his ideas, not as urging to reform, but as service in answer to need.

How Important Is Friendship?

The first and perpetual task for the community educator is to make himself personally acceptable to all with whom he proposes to work. Friendship is more important than the "correct" knowledge of next steps. It is probable that all good education rests upon inspiring personality, particularly in the learning which points toward adult maturity.

Part of the practitioner's role can be deliberately chosen. Part of it must be present in him and cannot be simulated. He must like people, like to be with them, like to see them grow. His preference for people appears both in cheerful tolerance for present limitations and in hopeful expectation of self-directed improvement.

The practitioner should circulate freely throughout the community, joining various organizations only as he can do so without excluding himself from others. He should convince people of his friendliness by listening with a sympathetic ear to their joys and woes. An ability to make intelligent comments on conversations heard, and an occasional humorous comment or good story all help. The establishment of himself as a good-intentioned person to be trusted should occur if possible before proposals for any new organization or activity are made. Time spent on cultivating friendship during a period of looking over the situation will pay off later.

One means for establishing friendship is sometimes difficult for students to understand. They, and perhaps many an adult, must be convinced that often the greatest kindness consists in accepting favors as well as giving them. People like those who are generous and thoughtful of their wishes. Generosity calls for giving things to friends, but it calls also for the enthusiastic receiving of offerings from these same friends. This is not always easy. It may mean accepting with joy some material object you do not want. The joy springs from appreciation of the spirit that prompted the gift. It may mean spending time at a party or on a visit at inconvenient hours. It may mean recognizing that some relatively valueless object, some ill-phrased approval represents the donor's most treasured possession or deepest compliment. And friendship calls for gracious and appreciative acceptance.

There is more in the act of acceptance of generosity than graciousness and fulsome expression of gratitude. By attaching importance to the giver's often humble gift you attach importance to him. You raise him a little above the level of the humble recipient of gifts. You begin the process of cultivating initiative in a future collaborator. The community educator must forever keep in mind the encouragement of generous impulses in the form which makes sense to the citizen. Friendliness means the sharing and mutual encouragement upon which trust and confidence can be built.

A warning: Friendliness has its hazards. So accustomed are men to living in a world of conflict and separated fragments that they find it difficult to believe that any one person can be universally friendly. The member of one faction will therefore often assume that the practitioner of sympathetic kindness is a member of his faith, simply because he does not argue or attempt to abuse that faith. Then when the practitioner is equally friendly with a rival faith, he may be accused of inconsistency or lack of loyalty. The genuine community educator continues his universal friendship in the expectation that such misunderstanding will not last forever.

Should Every Community Be Organized?

The answer is "No." Some assemblages of people may already have achieved a functioning unity which would easily be disrupted by unwise efforts to work out new organization. Some may have growth processes already in progress that point in the right direction. Others may not be ready for new steps because of failure in the recent past or because there is need to introduce the idea of over-all unity gradually to the emotional acceptance of people. Unfortunately there is no certain method for determining readiness in advance. An experienced community educator may offer an opinion from his wealth of background. But even he is often fooled, and the only sure test is the attempt to start processes pointing toward unity, then to see what happens.

The process starts with some activity which pulls people together in satisfying association. If some proposed activity can be found which seems to command widespread interest, the community is probably ready. If none can be found after diligent search, the prospect is not promising.

Most people, unaccustomed to thinking in terms of broad community growth, respond initially to proposed actions which meet their own individual needs. In one small town, the first activity which inspired general enthusiasm was a community chorus. Many of the individuals who came to practices faithfully pointed out that they received an emotional lift from the experience. The growing sense of over-all unity was, at best, secondary. When a project can be found that meets widespread individual need while making for unity, then a community is ready for organization.

What Is the Best Unit for Organization?

When unity is obviously lacking, the choice of territory and people to become a community is difficult. Before the days of the automobile and hard-surface highway, the rural village was a "natural" community. Is it now, or the township, or the consolidated school district, or the trade area around the county seat, or the territory around a center to which a majority of rural dwellers commute for work? In the city is the "proper" community a city block, neighborhood, political precinct, ward, or school district?

In the industrial era, people are seldom found in a "natural" or obvious community. Even if experts were wise enough to tell which conglomeration of people is best for development of a sense of belonging, it would be unwise to accept their advice. The question must be answered by the participants who achieve the unity. Their advance expectations, their loyalties modified by new experience are determining factors. The community educator should not make a choice of social unit without the aid of local advisers.

Is a Community Council Necessary?

If a new unity is sought, is a new organization necessary? Not always, although it is probably to be encouraged in a majority of situations. Sometimes an existing organization can broaden its interests to take on the first responsibilities of a council, a chamber of commerce (which will invite representation from other factions such as women's groups and organized labor), a conference of social agencies (if it will go beyond the professional social work point of view), a service club (provided there are no rivals to split loyalties). Such less-than-universal groupings can be used at the early stages with the hope that broader-based organization will be encouraged thereby.

A surer way to move toward the all-inclusiveness of a community council is to make use of widely representative committees on specific projects. A committee can be formed to promote construction of a swimming pool or improve relations between employer and employee. These bodies, endorsed and supported by existing organizations, can eventually point toward an over-all community council.

Decisions on such organizational matters must not be made by the community educator alone. He must work out practical steps with local advisers.

How Do You Choose a Beginning Project?

Men learn to plan for the general social good by finding satisfaction in planning first for limited, then for broader and broader, improvements. The selection of projects that start and continue the process calls for careful thought. The birth of a community council often awaits the conception of an idea that can become the starting project.

Which project to choose as a starter? The choice obviously rests upon the consciousness of need which exists or can be awakened. The community educator with his impatience will often choose some matter to which there is majority indifference. The importance of the activity to the practitioner is of less significance than the response of potential participants. Choose an activity which is likely to succeed, one which inspires little opposition. Resistance to controversial improvement will weaken with success in moving that which will move.

The choice of projects—the first one and all those to follow— should be made by local advisers, the freedom of decision of the educator diminishing as the responsibility of local people increases.

Local Contacts: Liabilities or Assets?

The community educator must work through and with other people. His success is limited by their limitations; he fails if he cannot stimulate them to bring to reality some of their latent potentialities. He is constantly dependent upon his interpretation of their descriptions of their own group life.

The practitioner, if outsider, is invited into the scene by people who probably have some special interest to promote. If a local person himself, he has some limited circle of friends who become advisers. In either case, he can press toward all-inclusive organization only if he recognizes that his initial contacts usually suffer from the narrow sympathies of fragmentary experience. Let him recognize also that he, himself, is probably a victim of the same ailment.

Decisions on next steps must be made in conferences of limited people. This is a characteristic of life. It need not worry anyone too much if the limited people are growing in the process. To develop situations which call for the growth of all concerned—that is the responsibility of the community educator.

The practitioner should form a circle of advisers even before any specific steps are taken, pointing toward organization. Starting as a small group, this should be expanded toward all-inclusiveness as rapidly as expansion of individual horizons will allow. Some of these persons, regrettably, may remain advisers only; the majority should become recruits for active participation in the improvement activities which will develop. Not only must the practitioner depend upon the advice of this expanding circle; he must depend upon many of them to take the initiative and become the ultimate leaders of social growth. By developing a long-suffering determination to work through others, he can turn local contacts into assets.

ACHIEVING UNITY

There are probably dozens of ways to achieve unity among the people inhabiting any small area. Among these, the formation of a community council frequently seems promising. If it can be assumed that a practitioner and his circle of advisers have agreed upon development of a council as desirable, the following are offered as suggestions. It should be reemphasized that he who reads to believe and apply faithfully has missed the point. No distillation of experience can be used in formula fashion to solve the problems of widely diverse situations.

What Is the First Step of Organization?

After a period of cultivation of people and digestion of ideas, the decision is reached to form a community council within a chosen area. An easily justified next step is the formation of an organizing committee. This is a normal expansion of, and an action taken by, the initial circle of advisers. It should point toward a wider inclusion of all elements. However, the organizing committee should spend a considerable amount of time inquiring into the probability that its outreach is still too narrow and should discover means for challenging the interest of groups not yet represented.

A vigorous organizing committee does much more than prepare the machinery of organization. It seeks out the justification for organization. It may spend weeks or months in open discussion of the need for a council, the possible jobs that might be undertaken, and the means for making representation as universal as possible. This period of informal conversational meetings may be prolonged the longer when there is doubt about the need for a council or when there is lack of cordiality and contact among represented organizations.

The organizing committee eventually brings forth a paper structure for the council. This, usually consisting of a constitution and bylaws, is presented as the formal proposal for setting up an organization. Sample constitutions are available from many sources but should be studied for ideas mainly. There is strength to be gained by study of forms of organization and by choice of rules in anticipation of difficulties that may arise. There are always legally minded folk about who lean heavily upon formal structure. But in our experience, no dying council was ever rescued by a good constitution, and strong councils are strong for reasons other than legal form. Adopt a constitution, yes, but do not expect it to do the job which only energetic members can do.

What About the Organizing Meeting?

The meeting for organization adopts the constitution. It also elects officers. The final obligation of the organizing committee is the selection of a slate of proposed officers. The slate selected by the committee will usually be elected *in toto* with occasionally the change of a name or two. So the responsibility of the organizing committee is heavy. This seeming power does not necessarily imply lack of democracy. It merely means that the experience of conscious self-direction is passed on, from those few who have the courage and insight to start things, to widening circles. Furthermore, democracy is not found in battles for the control of a voluntary organization. It is found in the greater and freer maturity of unity in the midst of understanding difference.

Should the organizing meeting be a big mass affair, with much publicity and the lift that the dramatic launching of a great public enterprise can give? No; on the whole, the organizing meeting should be quiet, a coming together of those already convinced or those willing to adventure with new experience. The meeting should be publicized and open to all interested but should not strive for the excitement of mass attendance. The great mass meeting is more consistent with the "selling" of preconceived ideas than with the quiet, unspectacular next achievements of ordinary mortals. In addition, a too exciting first meeting tends to bring forth thrilling promises of great things for the future, on the part of promoters. Then the fledgling council is bound and hampered by these expectations. It can be accused of failure if it falls short; it loses some of its freedom to explore the unexpected.

A date for the first meeting is chosen when the organizing committee is convinced that the maximum number of groups has been reached for cooperation. It is almost always necessary to assume that some clubs which should be a part of the enterprise will exclude themselves at the start. But formal organization should not be held up hoping for some reluctant doubters to be convinced by much eloquence. They will be more readily convinced by the actions that follow upon organization. Count on the pull of accomplishment to recruit the coy.

At the time of adoption of a constitution it is sometimes wise to determine the number of accredited representatives from each constituent group which will be allowed a vote. The hope is to build up the habit of making decisions by consensus rather than the division of a vote. But a limited voting power will tend to allay the fears of those who anticipate that the council may be dominated by some one faction which overwhelms meetings with its own followers. The purpose of legal safeguards is the clearing away of fears and hesitations in order to allow creative cooperation to grow.

Regular Meetings: How Often? For What?

There is a tendency on the part of amateur organizers to write into a constitution a compulsory listing of meetings, once every two weeks, once every month, or at some other designated interval. There is some wisdom in establishing regular habits of attendance (since so much of the rest of life is thus regimented by regular obligation), but no one should depend upon faithfulness to schedule, with fatal finality. People will give response to voluntary organizations less for the push of enforced obligation and more for the pull of vital interest. The fluctuations of interest and activity will be reflected in attendance. There should be some minimum limit to the number of meetings, possibly two to four per year, in order to keep the council alive. But for the rest of the time, frequency of meeting should be determined by the job at hand.

A fundamental purpose of meeting is the development of a warm atmosphere of mutual understanding in association together. This calls for former enemies or passing friends to see each other often, to confer together in the same room, with increasing mutual appreciation. But such enthusiasm for each other's presence does not arise from mere attendance. It comes rather from working together at some important job. Promote the job to be done more than the meeting.

What Committees Are Necessary?

Should a list of committees be set up in the constitution? For most community councils, this is doubtful practice. One is usually important—the executive committee, consisting frequently of officers, chairmen of other committees, and possibly some people elected at large. This group carries responsibility for decisions and actions in between meetings of the larger council. For the rest, committees can well be chosen as needed, continued as long as useful, and disbanded when their functions cease. There is a check on and a democratic discipline for their activity, or lack of activity, in reports to the meetings of the full council.

Committees are extremely important, so much so that they often seem to be the tail wagging the dog of the council. Frequently committee meetings will be better attended and livelier than those of the parent body. This is as it should be. But the over-all perspective of entire community need found in the council meeting is important. The committees also should be the instruments for spreading participation. The specific committee is the open door to the council for the reluctant.

What Happens to Constituent Organizations?

Does the functioning community council supersede or rival any constituent organization, actual or potential? No, not if properly run. The council coordinates the thinking of these fragmentary groups on issues of general welfare. It evolves broad plans into which the efforts of each separate group can fit. It assigns tasks, with the consent of the organization involved. The separate groups maintain their identity, strengthen themselves through service, and broaden their tolerance of one another and their understanding of general need.

The representatives on the council carry to its deliberations the points of view of their own fragmentary organizations. Ideally they report back the discussion and conclusions of council meetings. Unfortunately this referral does not occur as automatically as it should. It requires constant prodding to persuade representatives to meet their obligations. But only in the process of reporting back and forth can the council be kept from growing away from its member groups. Furthermore, the process of building up a corps of broad-gauge citizens is limited unless members of fragmentary groups can learn of contacts and experiences promoted by the council.

How to Conduct a Meeting

The meeting which brings people together in shared responsibility is the heart of the community growth process. The conduct of meetings is extremely important. Various manuals on this matter are available. These are helpful, but not too helpful. Most of them assume that the person addressed is chief operator, either as parliamentary chairman or as discussion leader. While the community educator will at times act in both capacities, he is making his strongest contribution when stimulating others to take the lead. Because no satisfactory manual exists covering the gentle art of encouraging leadership in others, the best advice that can be offered is to experiment with a policy of Suggest, Wait, and Act When the Group Is Ready.

The good community educator becomes a coach from the sidelines. He tries to keep meetings interesting by helping to plan challenging discussion. He encourages the timid to talk and the impatient and articulate to be patient with stumbling effort. He suggests ideas. He waits for others to come forward with proposals for action. When these are at all feasible (even though not as good as he would evolve) he offers enthusiastic support. This is not a process of seeking puppets to do his will. It is a process of encouraging people to have ideas and a will of their own. And his own desires should remain flexible, subject to the will of his cooperators.

What Do You Do When You Are Uncertain?

In general, the answer is "nothing." Wait and watch. Look for the birth of the spontaneous idea that can be supported.

UNITY IN ACTION

A true community council should never become an operating agency; it should be a broad planning body that pulls together and matures the best ideas of all. It keeps itself free from the complicated details of administration in order to cultivate unity for the general good.

Amateur Standing

In keeping with the demands of an age steeped in professional promotion, community leaders often call for the employment of an executive secretary as soon as a council is well set up. Such an employee can prove useful in carrying out routine duties that bore volunteers, in whipping up lagging interest. But it is easy for the council members as a whole to cast their burden of responsibility upon their hired agent. Then the important amateur flavor of the whole enterprise can be lost. If an executive secretary is employed, he should be watched lest he come to dominate. Council members should be watched even more lest they gladly surrender to such domination.

How to Finance a Council

In most organizations it is generally assumed that the bigger the budget, the better. In a community council a small budget is distinctly preferable. The smaller the annual expenditure, the easier it is to maintain a spirit of participation by ordinary citizens. The actual amount must be determined by the council membership in terms of size of community, responsibilities undertaken, whether officers are employed, and whether a rented headquarters is maintained. If expenditures can be held to such simple matters as cost of mail, phone calls, and a few trips for council members to obtain information, the budget can be modest.

The raising of money is obviously simpler with a small contemplated expenditure. Frequently the modest monthly or annual contributions of member organizations will meet limited needs. These can be supplemented by contributions from a few interested individuals as long as the council does not become obligated for such generosity. When, however, a council budget has become sufficiently large to require a financial drive or campaign to obtain necessary support, the council is threatened with loss of its citizen-planning and amateur function.

How to Finance the Expensive Project

No condemnation of the great financial drive is intended. This is apparently a permanent feature of American life, regarded as desirable by benefiting public service agencies and as necessary by a contributing public. There are widely experienced directors of such enterprises with a recognized body of accepted practice who can be professionally employed.

When some specific and expensive project has been selected as a next step in community progress, the drive to raise money for its completion should be turned over to a church, a Y.M.C.A., a service club, in cooperation with plans of the council. If need be, a separate agency to finance and operate can be set up with full legal organization of incorporation and a board of trustees. But the council should fulfill its function by remaining free to maintain a broad view of changing community need. It should work for a warmth of togetherness rather than an efficiency of money raising.

What Is the Relationship to Government?

Even as a community council remains free from private financial and administrative detail, it avoids involvement with government, either local or distant. Public officials may be members of the council, but as citizens, not as voices of authority. The amateur planning efforts of citizens must remain unhampered to recommend, and criticize, according to discovered need, not according to political expediency.

Government in a democracy responds to pressure. A community council can become one of the pressuring bodies, calling for the election of better officials or mobilizing public sentiment to gain support for certain improvements. But this activity does not represent responsible citizens at their mature best. A conferring with public employees to seek solution of problems is more representative of the dignity of responsibility. Frequently the best way to overcome governmental apathy is to start some project, even on small scale, that draws attention to a neglected problem. Tax money can often be made available to carry on an activity which was begun on small scale or financed initially by privately raised funds. An active community council can afford to be venturesome, passing along an enterprise to more conservative government hands when it has proved its worth. The important matter is that citizens growing in the maturing experience of a community council avoid becoming subservient to their elected officials and avoid attempting to dominate them. They gain self-confidence by learning to work as dignified citizens, capable of thinking through problems with either the expertly informed or the politically powerful.

EVEN GOOD THINGS COME TO AN END

No community organization is immortal. This fact is not always tragic, though the enthusiastic promoter who vainly applies all manner of restoratives to an ailing council may well conclude that death ends all hope.

What to Do in Periods of Waning Enthusiasm

A council at a low ebb of enthusiasm and activity does not necessarily promise an early end. Fluctuations of vigor are the normal lot of men, both as individuals and as organizations. The wise practitioner is the one who calmly anticipates periods of quiescence. Some such periods occur each year—say, during the Christmas season or in the summer—unless there is some vigorous vacation activity. Other slack seasons come after the completion of successful projects. What to do? Suggest and wait. Be prepared to leap into enthusiastic support when a good idea is proposed. The promoter must not allow himself to go to sleep or become discouraged. He must be ready to turn on his enthusiasm when the situation calls for it.

Should meetings be canceled during a period of feeble enthusiasm? No. They may be allowed to occur less often but should not be dropped even though only a handful attend. For it is in the meeting that the spark of a new project may appear. The life of a council moves from project to project until enthusiasm for general welfare planning develops.

Should a Failure Ever Be Allowed?

Sometimes a practitioner may stand by and allow a council to achieve a minor failure, by way of a lesson. This is a vigorous kind of shock treatment. Most experienced community educators will advise against such strong medicine, pointing out that failure will occur often enough despite all best efforts. It is better to abandon a project than allow it to move on to probable disappointment. If an abandonment is necessary, try to bring in a substitute activity quickly.

How to Handle the Failure That Cannot Be Avoided

Sometimes, despite warnings, a council goes on with an activity foredoomed to frustration. Sometimes all involved, including the practitioner, make a mistake in judgment and months of effort prove futile. Then what? A paralyzing discouragement may result. Or there may occur a period of mutual blaming and backbiting. Or the council may achieve an objectivity to analyze causes and go on to correct failures. The patient practitioner seeks this latter outcome in continuing meetings, pointing toward renewed activity as rapidly as possible.

If the council does not survive the shock of failure, an attempt can be made to rescue the essentials of a sense of community. After the disappointment of disintegration has passed, it may be found that other organizations have taken up some of the task of general planning and promotion of community solidarity.

The death of a favorite council does not necessarily mean that all is lost. The wise practitioner does not attempt to revive a moribund organization. He merely accepts an uncomfortable fact and goes on. Life is dynamic. The inevitability of change is welcome news to those who realize that improvement is always possible. The successful practitioner is the one who recognizes that not even failure is immortal. He keeps flexible for another try when the time is ripe.

When the pain of frustrated effort has yielded to a more philosophic calm, it will often be found that a collapsed community effort has left an unexpected dividend of positive results. A new crop of leaders has matured which is harvested by many desirable enterprises. Certain organizations already in existence will change and broaden their functions to include a wider definition of public welfare. A stronger and more real sense of togetherness may have developed; new friendships are created. A hunger for a more satisfying and inclusive community life may have arisen in many, one which promises well for the next enterprise in search of unity. Some new form of organization may eventually be found to satisfy that hunger.

Should Permanent Organization Be Sought?

The successful practitioner is not the one who develops a powerful, permanent organization to perpetuate his name. Let the wealthy, highly organized groups with paid promoters seek immortality. The community educator pursues more subtle and, we believe, more significant ends.

Community councils need periodic renewal. Like all human institutions, they tend toward an organizational hardening of the arteries. They need new blood, new personalities, preferably from among those who have not as yet had the experience of leadership. This renewal can come by recruitment of those new to responsibility, to replace those grown gray. Or it may take the form of new organizations when the old are no longer useful. The favorable outcome is not stronger institutions but better people.

WHAT IS OF PERMANENT VALUE?

The lack of spectacular results, slowness of progress, and impermanence of institution can easily discourage the unsophisticated community practitioner. He often finds himself apologetic before friends who measure success in terms of gigantism, headline-hunting excitement, and material construction. He must be clear enough in his own objectives to measure his success in terms of psychological residues. Whatever happens to community councils or to the specific projects they promote, the outcome of permanent significance is found in the changed lives of people.

Anyone who proposes to help people help themselves needs to adjust his sights in a paradoxical fashion. For immediate results, the next possible steps, he needs to lower his expectations. For long-range results, the continuing growth of individuals, he needs to raise his sights to unlimited horizons. The developmental possibilities of men are beyond prediction of present understanding. But these potentialities will be realized by multiplied forward steps, each of which will seem minor at the time it is taken.

The ultimate evaluation of programs of community improvement lies not in what happens to a community. It lies in what happens to the people who live in it. Do they become responsibly stronger leaders of their own lives, of each other, of their collective life?

The College as Practitioner

Could an institution become a community practitioner? The small college becomes community educator for small towns. Though citizens may accept the college as if it possessed a single collective personality, such an idea does violence both to psychological understanding and to the separate personalities who all together compose the college. The better concept is that a college might cultivate a multitude of practitioners on its staff who could raise the level of community responsibility and of democratic leadership for a region small in size but significant in influence.

No greater challenge can come to the small college than to be the inspirer of a new breed of leadership for maturing democracy. To continue training future leaders among students, yes, but to make them even more promising by letting them join in the college's endeavor to collaborate in the self-educative activities of maturing citizens at the small-town roots of democracy—that can make the small college unique.

Appendix

A List of Helps
for
Responsible Citizens, Community Educators, and Educators
of Community Educators

There is a growing mass of material in the fields of community development, human relations, group dynamics, and related fields of interest for community educators and leaders. Any list is foredoomed to be "dated" shortly after it is published. We present herewith, not a complete list of useful titles, not a full coverage of those materials which have inspired our work, but some sources of help which might be offered as a starting point for those wishing to pursue study of references.

These helps include books, pamphlets, magazines, and organizations. The sources of help are arranged according to a classification suggested by the kind of inquiry which has come to us. Assignments to a particular heading of the classification may seem arbitrary, at times, since one book may cover several different emphases, or might be otherwise placed according to point of view. A brief annotation or comment is offered to give a hint of our judgment as to utility.

Philosophic Statements. The general problem of the community in modern times.

Brownell, Baker, *The Human Community*, Harper, New York, 1950, 296 pages.
   A philosophical treatise on various aspects of small-community life based upon the author's work in the "Montana Study." A classic on fundamental theory. Many valuable suggestions but not a handbook. Especially for thoughtful readers.

Brownell, Baker, *The College and the Community*, Harper, New York, 1952, 248 pages.
   A challenge to colleges to accept responsibility for community growth. It often makes the orthodox educator uncomfortable. Is this present book a partial answer to the challenge?

Hayes, Wayland J., *The Small Community Looks Ahead*, Harcourt, Brace, New York, 1947, 275 pages.
   A review of processes and achievements of the emerging "community

movement." Gives several planning-to-action sequences. Easy reading. Good bibliography.

Lilienthal, David E., *TVA—Democracy on the March*, Harper, New York, 1944, 248 pages.

An easily read account of the early days of the TVA development as an encourager of local community democracy. Almost a classic. Describes in theory and practice how planning can be carried on by ordinary people to strengthen themselves.

Morgan, Arthur E., *The Small Community, Foundation of Democratic Life*, Harper, New York, 1942, 312 pages.

Out of a broad experience as engineer, educator, and organizer of a community service agency, the author distills his faith in the basic character of small-town life, with recommendations on how this is to be recaptured in modern industrial times.

Practical Handbooks. General all-round guides.

Haiman, Franklyn S., *Group Leadership and Democratic Action*, Houghton Mifflin, Boston, 1951, 309 pages.

A handbook on how to get along with people in the setting of democratic action.

Hillman, Arthur, *Community Organization and Planning*, Macmillan, New York, 1950, 378 pages.

A textbook bringing together the ideas of community organization (usually monopolized by sociologists and social workers) and planning (usually monopolized by architects and engineers). Depends heavily upon quotations.

Sanders, Irwin T., *Making Good Communities Better*, University of Kentucky Press, Lexington, Ky., 1950, 174 pages.

Probably the best single all-round handbook now available, described by the author as a "headbook." Readable and useful.

The Art of Working with People in Groups. There is a wealth of material in this field. The few titles suggested are especially useful and up to date.

Bergevin, Paul, and Morris, Dwight, *Group Processes for Adult Education*, University of Indiana, Bloomington, Ind., 1952, 86 pages.

A pamphlet describing various kinds of meetings and how they may be handled to produce concrete results.

Hall, D. M., *The Dynamics of Group Discussion*, The Interstate Printers, 19-27 N. Jackson Street, Danville, Ill., 1950, 63 pages.

A pamphlet offering practical guidance to discussion leaders. One of the best.

Journal of Social Issues, Association Press, 291 Broadway, New York 7, N. Y.

A quarterly publication of the Society for the Psychological Study of Social Issues. Keeps abreast of thinking in the field of group dynamics.

Let's Have a Discussion, League of Women Voters of the U.S.A., 1026-17th Street, N.W., Washington 6, D.C., 1950, 8 pages.
A brief but pithy pamphlet. The L. W. V. has many practical helps on a wide variety of subjects.

Lippitt, Ronald, *Training in Community Relations*, Harper, New York, 1949, 286 pages.
An account of leadership training by conferences and workshop sessions. The author, an exponent of group dynamics, leans more toward training techniques than toward experience.

Research. By experts and by ordinary citizens.

Colcord, Joanna, *Your Community*, Russell Sage Foundation, New York, rev. ed., 1947, 263 pages.
The type of information about a community that might be assembled by citizens as part of a self-analysis.

Jahoda, Marie, Deutsch, Morton, and Cook, Stuart W., *Research Methods in Social Relations*, Dryden, New York, 1951, 2 vols., 759 pages.
Two volumes giving an excellent summary of scientific viewpoints and methods on social research. Very technical, for those who want such heavy material.

Your Community Looks at Itself, The New South, Southern Regional Council, 63 Auburn Avenue, N.E., Atlanta 3, Ga., 63 pages.
A pamphlet "Manual for the Home Town Self-Survey." The complete outline of topics with suggested questions.

Education and Community Processes. Elementary school, high school, college, adult education.

Annual Reports, Program of Community Dynamics, Earlham College, Richmond, Ind.
Published annually, showing growth from uncertain beginnings and continuing into the future.

Bridges Between School and the Community, junior high schools and grades seven and eight of elementary schools, New York City Board of Education, 1949, 79 pages.
Simple, anecdotal descriptions of projects in schools of the nation's largest city.

Essert, Paul L., *Creative Leadership of Adult Education*, Prentice-Hall, New York, 1951, 333 pages.
Adult education swings away from classes toward the development of citizens in community action.

Hart, Joseph K., *Education in the Humane Community*, Harper, New York, 1951, 168 pages.
The final writings of a pioneer in education and community growth. Philosophic and challenging, but does not offer suggestions for next steps.

McClaren, W. K., *Selected Community School Programs in the South,* George Peabody College for Teachers, Nashville, Tenn., 1948, 216 pages.
Case reports on twenty-two schools whose programs are community centered. Small towns especially.

Olsen, Edward G., *School and Community Programs,* Prentice-Hall, New York, 1949, 509 pages.
Source book of successful community-school projects. All age levels.

The Responsibility of the Churches.

Dana, M., *The Larger Parish Plan,* Congregational Church Extension Boards, New York City.
Description of how rural religion can strengthen services by combining weak churches into a united effort.

Ligutti and Rawe, *Rural Roads to Security,* Bruce Publishing Co., Milwaukee, Wis., 1940.

Lindstrom, David E., *Rural Life and the Church,* The Garrard Press, Champaign, Ill., 1946, 205 pages.
A careful judgment on the role of the church in rural life by a major authority. Not easy reading.

Manifesto on Rural Life, National Catholic Rural Life Conference, Bruce Publishing Co., Milwaukee, Wis., 1944, 222 pages.
Principles and policies of the Roman Catholic Church on rural life. Bases for solution of problems, not the solutions. For this see Ligutti and Rawe, above.

Smith, Rockwell C., *The Church in Our Town,* Abingdon-Cokesbury, Nashville, Tenn., 1945, 190 pages.
Covers functioning of churches, but also methods of organizing small-town communities. Readable and even inspiring.

Planning, a Job for Ordinary Citizens. Most of the material on planning is addressed to such experts as engineers, architects, and public officials. A few humbler suggestions are these:

ASPO Newsletter, 1313 East 16th Street, Chicago 37, Ill.
The official publication of the American Society of Planning Officials. A monthly addressed to professional planners but sometimes containing material of interest to ordinary mortals.

Black, Russell Van Nest, *Planning for the Small American City,* Public Administration Service, Publication No. 87, Chicago, Ill., 1944, 86 pages.
A simple but complete handbook of planning for the average citizen. Almost a classic.

King, Clarence, *Organizing for Community Action,* Harper, New York, 1948, 202 pages.
This could have been listed among the handbooks. It is put here to indi-

cate a method for pulling communities together to plan. Easy to read;
good case stories.

Know Your Town's Future, National League of Women Voters, 1026-17th
Street, N.W., Washington 6, D. C., 34 pages.
    Another good L.W.V. pamphlet. The factors that need to be taken into
    consideration in planning.

Communities in Action. Many titles under other headings cover action.
These few are especially good for a wide range of interests.

Dahir, James, *Communities for Better Living,* Harper, New York, 1950,
321 pages.
    A complete coverage of community development activities in many cities
    of the U.S.A. Case material, well classified and well analyzed.

Extension Division Bulletin, University of Virginia, Charlottesville, Va.
    A monthly publication giving in brief form the story of some community
    in process of solving its own problems. Readable and helpful.

The People Act Radio Series, The People Act Center, State College, Penna.
    A radio program telling the story of specific communities where people
    worked toward solution of their own problems. Both printed and
    recorded copies of broadcasts are available as well as helps for those
    who write in to the Center in State College, Pa.

Recreation Activities.

Butler, G. D., *Introduction to Community Recreation.* McGraw-Hill, New
York, 1940, 547 pages.
    An encyclopedia of recreation, philosophy, leadership, organization, ad-
    ministration. How it all relates to planning. Prepared under sponsorship
    of the National Recreation Association.

Gardner, Ella, *Handbook for Recreation Leaders,* Children's Bureau, U.S.
Government Printing Office, Washington, D. C., 1948, 121 pages.
    Excellent, inexpensive handbook of games, drama, music, and so on.
    Especially addressed to the untrained leader.

Know Your Community, National Recreation Association, New York.
    One of many brief pamphlets published by this association. Good to stir
    interest.

Health as a Community Matter.

Health and Welfare Planning in the Smaller Community, Community
Chests and Councils, Inc., 155 E. 44th Street, New York, 1945, 27 pages.
    Pamphlet with suggestions on things that might be done by amateur
    citizen interest.

Hiscock, Ira V., *Ways to Community Health Education,* Commonwealth Fund, New York, 1939.
A description of standard public relations practice applied to the health field. How to "put over" a campaign of publicity for a good cause.

Housing Problems. How action in this field may contribute to citizen growth.

Colbert, R. J., *Guide to Community Action on a Local Program for Building and Construction,* University of Wisconsin Extension Division, Madison, Wis., 1945.
One of several publications by this university in a number of fields. Good as a guide to housing activities.
Festinger, Schachter, and Back, *Social Pressures in Informal Groups,* Harper, New York, 1950, 240 pages.
Summary of a successful action-research project in a housing situation.
Marrow, Alfred J., *Living Without Hate,* Harper, New York, 1951, 269 pages.
A significant and readable account of another action-research project in a housing development. Problem: to reduce bigotry. Good case material.
Mutual Housing, U.S. Office of the Housing Expediter, U.S. Government Printing Office, Washington, D. C., 1946, 55 pages.
A pamphlet giving practical advice on organizing, financing, constructing, operating, and managing a mutual housing association. Addressed mainly to veterans, but useful for others as well.

The Small Town, Its Hopes and Limitations.

Community Service News, Yellow Springs, Ohio.
A quarterly publication devoted to new life for the small town. Community Services, Inc., which produces this small but significant journal, has other publications to recommend and will help local communities on specific problems.
Ogden, Jean and Jess, *Small Communities in Action,* Harper, New York, 1946, 244 pages.
Thirty-four stories from small communities.
Ogden, Jean and Jess, *These Things We Tried,* University of Virginia, Charlottesville, Va., 1947, 432 pages.
University of Virginia's experimented program. Especially useful is Part 4, "Ways That Have Worked—or Have Not."
Poston, Richard, *Small Town Renaissance,* Harper, New York, 1950, 241 pages.
A narrative description of small-town possibilities, taken from experience in the "Montana Study." Readable and inspiring.

West, James, *Plainville, U. S. A.,* Columbia University Press, 1945, 238 pages.

The problems of an isolated and backward rural community responding to urban influences. Problems, not solutions.

The Big City. Can community life be found in such a place?

Alinsky, Saul, *Reveille for Radicals,* University of Chicago Press, Chicago, 1946, 228 pages.

The organization of the "Back of the Yards" council in Chicago, in a seemingly hopeless slum section. The author believes in using "natural" leaders to promote good causes.

Peterson, Elmer (ed.), *Cities Are Abnormal,* University of Oklahoma Press, Norman, Okla., 1946, 263 pages.

A symposium of fourteen articles on what is wrong with city life. Problems, with only fanciful solutions.

Thorndike, E. L., *Your City.* Harcourt, Brace, New York, 1939, 204 pages.

Results of a study of 310 American cities. Gives the things to look for in making a city good, but offers no suggestions on what to do.

Wittenberg, Rudolph, *The Art of Group Discipline. A Mental Hygiene Approach to Leadership,* Association Press, New York, 1951, 124 pages.

A description of the "block organization" in New York City. An experiment with the rediscovery of community spirit in the press of a great city.

Conflict and How to Move Toward Integration.

Chase, Stuart, *Roads to Agreement,* Harper, New York, 1951, 250 pages.

A "journey of exploration" into a number of fields to discover useful and practical techniques for bringing harmony out of conflict.

Group Tensions in the United States, The American Association of University Women, 1634 Eye Street, N.W., Washington 6, D.C.

An outline pamphlet for community study. The A.A.U.W. has many pamphlets on a variety of subjects. Most of these are helpful to community practitioners.

Lasker, Bruno, *Democracy Through Discussion,* H. W. Wilson, New York, 1949, 368 pages.

A thorough analysis of discussion processes looking toward mediation.

Lewin, Kurt, *Resolving Social Conflicts,* Harper, New York, 1948, 230 pages.

A collection of profound and thoughtful writings by a psychologist and founder of the group dynamics school of thought. The experimental approach.

Utterback, William E., *Decision Through Discussion,* The Ohio State University Discussion Service, 205 Derby Hall, Ohio State University, Columbus, Ohio, 1948.

A short pamphlet on discussion leading to integration. The Discussion

Service of Ohio State University publishes material regularly on the discussion process. Helpful for amateurs.

Walser, Frank, *The Art of Conference,* Harper, New York, 1948.
How conferences can be used to inform and to get things done.

Watson, Goodwin B., *Action for Unity,* Harper, New York, 1947, 165 pages.
Review of efforts in the United States to improve interfaith and interracial relations. Good overview, but lacking details.

Work Camps and How They Work.

American Friends Service Committee, 20 South 12th Street, Philadelphia, Penna., has a number of pamphlets on work camping:
> *Voluntary Work Camp, A New Instrument of Education.*
> *Work and Contemplation,* by Douglas Steere.
> *Week-End Work Camping,* by David Ritchie.

Begert, Willy, *Organizing International Voluntary Work Camps,* UNESCO, 19 Avenue Kleber, Paris, France.
A practical handbook on the organization, setup, and scheduling of work camps. Especially related to international good will, but can be applied equally well to community good will.

Best and Pike, *International Voluntary Service for Peace. A History, 1920-1946,* Allen and Unwin, London, 1948.
A history of the work camp movement from beginnings in First World War.

Holland, Kenneth, *Work Camps for College Students,* American Council of Education, Washington, D. C., 1941.
The setup and philosophy of work camping.

The Economic Base for Community Life. Almost all writings on the economics of local situations discuss effects upon community life—for better or for worse. The following titles are significant for the economics of self-help and local automony.

Coady, M. M., *Masters of Their Own Destiny,* Harper, New York, 1939, 170 pages.
How the development of cooperatives raised the whole level of living and of community life in Nova Scotia.

Morgan, Arthur, *Small Community Economics,* Fellowship Publications, New York, 1943, 44 pages.
Rural communities must offer more than a single occupation (farming). Another publication, *A Business of My Own,* by the same author is available from Community Services, Inc., Yellow Springs, Ohio.

Voorhis, Jerry, *How to Organize a Coop,* Cooperative League of the U.S.A., Chicago, Ill., 1948, 34 pages.
Handbook on organization of cooperative stores, credit unions, and so

on. An official publication of the Cooperative League, which has other
materials available.

Community Development in Other Cultures.

UNESCO Courier, Unesco House, 19 Avenue Kleber, Paris, France.
A monthly international periodical. Especially interested in problems of
"fundamental education," the removal of illiteracy and the achieving of
basic habits of health and cooperation. UNESCO is moving more and
more toward the "village approach."

The Work of the Division of Community Education, Department of Education of Puerto Rico, San Juan, P.R., 1952.
A mimeographed report of a significant development among a Spanish-
speaking people. Applying a philosophy of self-help community building
on large scale. Other publications are available from the Division or its
director, Mr. Fred Wale.

Index

Abundance, shared, 166
Action-research, 76-78, 136
Adult education, 40-1, 61
Advisors, local, 180
Agreement, technique of, 109-11
Amateurs, 41, 55-56, 184
Annual report, 150
Apathy, 39, 43, 103, 112, 157-8
Argument as persuasion, 87
Assistance to underprivileged people, 131-2, 133
Atmosphere, permissive, 109-11
Atmosphere, social, 94 ff, 109

"Bag of Tricks," avoidance of, 174
Beginning project, choice of, 178
Belonging, sense of, 157
Bible, 84, 112
Brethren, Church of, 128
Bunche, Ralph, 112

Catharsis, 109-10
Catholics, 128, 154
Celebrities, 2-3
Challenge to small college, 189
Challenge to social scientists, 150-1
Chamber of Commerce, 178
Churches, 2, 46, 105, 128-9, 145, 153-4
City planning, 61
Committees, importance of, 182
Communism, 91, 101
Communities, changes in small, 32 ff, 36
Community Chest, 6, 156
Community, choice of unit, 177
Community Council, 47 ff, 143, 177-8
Community, definition of, 29 ff
  evaluation by, 20, 23

Community—*Continued*
  request from, 21
  sense of, 31, 162
  size of, 37
Community education, 38-9
Community educator, 7-8, 73
Community integration, 154
Community organization, 176-7
Community organizer, 6-7
Community relationships to college, 19-20
Competition, social, 158-9
Compromise, 114-5
Consensus, 71-2, 105-7
Conciliators, 107 ff, 113-4
Conference of Social Agencies, 178
Confidence, creation of, 78
Constitution, legal form of, 180
Cooperation, creative, 165
Creative agreement, 107
Creative disagreement, 102
Criticism, acceptance of, 172

Death of a community council, 187-8
Decentralization, 36
Defense from worry, 171
Defensive reactions against change, 167
Democracy, process of becoming, 148-9
Democracy and complacency, 67
Democratic discipline based on social purposes, 146
Democratic discipline, self-imposed, 145
Development of self-confidence in citizens, 52-3
Dictatorship, 58, 68
Differences, superficial, 148
Dignity of individual, 157, 186
Diplomacy, 79, 82-3

Direct action in reform, 173
Directness in dealing with people, 173
Discretion, achievement of, 69
Discussion, 63-4
  as promotion, 66, 125
  post-analysis of, 65
  pre-analysis of, 65
Doubters, How Handled, 54-5, 181

Education, definition of, 38
Education, liberal arts, 13
Emerson, Ralph Waldo, 121
Episcopalians, 128
Evaluations of program, 19-20, 23
Evaluation in lives of participants, 162,
  188-9
Events as persuasion, 88-9
Expanding interests, 51-2
Experiment, need for, 162-3
Experts, 3, 39

Factionalism, 103-4
Failure, causes and responses, 163-4
Failure, definition of, 163
  what to do about, 187-8
Father-substitute, 3-4
Fear, deterrent to cooperation, 165, 181
Fear of reason, 141-2
Financial contribution, 124
Financing a community council, 184-5
Financing a major project, 185
Flexibility, 134
Fluctuations in enthusiasm, 49-50, 186-7
Fragments, social, 157-8, 183
Frame of reference, 147
Freedom vs. group control, 152-3
Freedom achieved by control of group,
  155
Friendliness, hazards of, 176
Friendship, 175-6

Generalists, 74
Generosity, acceptance of, 176
Goodwill, faith in, 129
  and enthusiasm, 126-7
  and normality, 124
  humble, 93
  voluntary, 159-60
Grading by teachers, 59
Graduate students, 18

Greatness, humble, 57
Grievances, forum for, 110-11, 161

Health activities, 61
Helplessness, sense of, 155-6, 159
Humor, sense of, 70-1, 171
"Hunch" in social situations, 99, 110
Hypotheses developed from experience,
  138-9

Idealism, discipline of, 67-8
Immaturity, disorganized, 142-3
Indoctrination, 86
Inflexible righteousness, 114-5
Influencing group atmosphere, 95-7,
  104-5
  limitations of, 98
Institutional coercions, 158-9
Intelligent listening, 78-9
Inter-racial cooperation, 44, 47, 62, 75

Jews, 154

Kellogg, Charles W., 165
Kingdom of Heaven, 2

Laboratories, foreign, 27-8
  rural, 26-7
  urban, 26
Leadership principle, 3
Learning attitude, 85, 143
Learning, mutual, 40-1, 173
Learning, process of discovery in, 149
Limited people, dependence upon, 179
Lobbying, 156-7, 162, 186
Loyalty to social fragments, 158
Lutherans, 154

Manipulation, social, 5-6, 81-2
Mass communication, 87 ff, 90, 94
Mass meeting, 47, 181
Maturity, growth toward, 143
Meaning vs. coercion, 159-60
Meetings and democratic processes,
  62 ff, 182
Meetings, conduct of, 183-4
Methodists, 128, 154
Millennium, 154
Mistakes, making assets of, 170
Motivation, 92-3

"Natural" leaders, 4-5
Need, discovery of, 143

Neighborhood council, 45
Neutral counsellor, 108, 114, 117-8
News, interpretation of, 89, 102
Nobility, avoidance of, 83-4, 172

Objectivity, collective, 140, 142
Objectivity and security, 140
Objectivity as self-discipline, 69, 139
"Old Adam" theory, 91
Oppositions, dissolving, 167
Organizing committee, 180
Organizing meeting, 180-1
Overorganization, 35

Parallel responsibilities, 56
Participant-leaders, 8-9, 37-8
Participant observer, 136
Patience for change, 148-9, 170
Planning, participation by ordinary people, 132
Political relations, 185-6
Post-community, 31, 35
Practitioner, definition of, 169
    motto of, 170
    role of, 175
Pre-community, 31, 35
Presbyterians, 128
Press cooperation, 47, 119 ff, 122-3
Production potential, 165-6
Propaganda, 6-7, 87 ff
Protestants, 154
Public relations, 120
    usefulness of students in, 133
Publicity for goodwill, 121-2
"Pure" scientist, 10, 136, 144

Quakers, 13, 107

Radio and press, 116
Radio news commentators, 89
Readiness for growth, 48
Readiness for organization, 176-7
Readiness to learn, 143
Records, 23-4
Recreation activities, 48, 60-1, 153
Regression in maturity, 173
Religious orthodoxy, 136
Renewal of organization, 188
Reporters as educators, 119-20, 122-3
Research, use of references in, 65-6
    response of subjects in, 135-6

Results, unspectacular, 188
Roosevelt, Franklin Delano, 1

Salesman for good causes, 74
Scapegoat minority, 34-5
Scheduling service activities, 18-9
Science, definition of, 10-11
    experimentation in, 9-10
    for ordinary people, 9-10
    methods of, learned in action, 76-7
    ordinary citizen as contributor to, 143-4
Scientific guessing, 136 ff
Secrecy in negotiation, 116-7
Seeking out problems, 173-4
Self-effacement, 79-80, 97-8, 171
Self-investigation, 143-4, 149-50
Self-investigation a continuing process, 145
Self-observation, 98
Self-persuasion, 94
Seminar in community problems, 14 ff
Separateness and need for togetherness, 167-8
Service club, 178
Spokesman, problem of, 112
Spreading participation, 125-6, 127-8
Success and failure, incidents in process of, 163 ff, 171-2
Success, definition and response, 164-5
Suffering, 111-2
Survival of community association, 161-162

Technical assistance programs, 133
Technical "know-how," 166
Tentativeness of conclusions, 138
Timing, art of, 80-1

Uncertainty, what to do in case of, 184
Uncertainty as contributor to education, 129, 132-3
Understanding, cultivation of, 146-7, 171

Wholeness, experience of, 160
Wonder, ability to, 174
Work camps, 16, 127, 131 ff
Worry, 171

Y.M.C.A., 156, 185

Set in Linotype Baskerville
Format by Marguerite Swanton
Manufactured by The Haddon Craftsmen, Inc.
Published by HARPER & BROTHERS, *New York*